QUICK 'N' EASY
WEB PAGES

DAVE'S QUICK 'N' EASY WEB PAGES

AN INTRODUCTORY GUIDE TO CREATING WEB SITES

written by
Dave Lindsay

illustrated by
Sean Lindsay

edited by
Bruce Lindsay

Erin Publications
Calgary, Canada
2001

Second Edition, 2001

ISBN 0-9690609-8-X

Printed in Canada

All terms mentioned in this book that are known to be trademarks or service marks have been capitalized. The publisher cannot attest to the accuracy of this information. Use of a term in this book should not be regarded as affecting the validity of any trademark or service mark.

Canadian Cataloguing in Publication Data

Lindsay, Dave, 1984-
    Dave's quick 'n' easy web pages : an introductory guide to creating web sites

2nd ed.
Includes index.
ISBN 0-9690609-8-X

    1. Web sites--Design. 2. HTML (Document markup language). I. Lindsay, Bruce, 1949- II. Title. III. Title: Dave's quick and easy web pages. IV. Title: Quick 'n' easy web pages.
TK5105.888.L55 2001   005.7'2   C00-900894-2

Erin Publications
82 Edenstone View NW
Calgary, AB   T3A 4T5
Canada

E-mail: info@erinbooks.com
Web site: http://www.erinbooks.com

Foreword

Almost three years ago while on a whirlwind tour of Canada I had the great pleasure of meeting David Lindsay.

He had written to me to tell me how much he loved my books and to ask me if he could start a Redwall club on the 'net.

I was charmed and intrigued.

Charmed because of his wonderful enthusiasm and intrigued by the idea of the 'net. Of course I agreed and so The Official Redwall Club came into being.

Being a technophobe I know nothing about the techniques used to make these wonderful pages. I see only the results. An amazing world wide connection between myself and my readers where we can talk and exchange ideas.

A warm and close family of Redwall readers is even closer because of David, his dad Bruce, and his brother Sean. How is it done? Now you can find out, they are going to share the knowledge and expertise... what sterling chaps!!

I wish them all the success they deserve and recommend their book wholeheartedly.

Brian Jacques

Contents

Introduction

My goal in writing this book is to make web publishing accessible to as many people around the world as possible. This book shows how to create a web site without spending any money. I've explained the process as simply as I can. Where there are several ways to accomplish a task, I've described the easiest way I know.

Though many beginners rely on HTML editors, I don't recommend them. I believe that to be successful, web publishers must understand the HTML coding process. An HTML editor is a helpful tool for a web publisher the same way a calculator is a helpful tool for an engineer, but if you don't understand the basics, you're limiting yourself. Once you understand how HTML works you'll be able to learn and use new web page techniques as soon as you see them. When you discover a new web page trick on someone else's web page you can look at the source code to see how it's done, then add something similar to your own web page. Knowing HTML also allows you to make last minute modifications to your web page when you're uploading a file to the server.

HTML is easy to learn and easy to use. You can write HTML in a text editor in DOS (Edit), in Windows (Notepad), on a Mac (Simpletext or BBEdit), in Linux (pico or emacs), or in UNIX (pico or emacs). You can use a word processor too, if you save your files in ASCII format. I use Windows Notepad to write HTML. It's easy to use and it saves the files in ASCII.

You can set up your web site entirely for free. You should be able to get free Internet access through your school or public library. If that's not possible, you can obtain it from one of the many Internet Service Providers (ISPs) sponsored by advertisers. Appendix B tells where to find these ISPs. Appendix D shows where to find free web server space.

The next step is to install the latest version of the browser you'd like to use. Netscape Communicator and Internet Explorer are the two most popular choices. They're both free. Instead of including them on a CD of shareware which quickly becomes outdated, I've shown how to download the latest versions of all the software you'll need, free from the Internet. Check Appendix A to obtain the browser of your choice.

If you're a "newbie" start with Chapter 1. You can create your first web page and upload it to the Internet in a couple of hours at most. You'll be able to see results right away. Then add extra features using Chapters 2 to 13. These chapters are set up in a logical order, but once Chapter 1 is completed you can jump to any chapter in any order you'd like.

If you already have some experience with HTML you can go directly to the topics you're interested in and read just what you need. The Table of Contents and the Index will help you quickly find the tip or trick you're looking for. Non-HTML information can be found in Appendices at the back of this book together with a Glossary which will explain any terms you're not familiar with.

All HTML code in this book is shown in bold capital letters to make it easier to recognize. However, a friend at the World Wide Web Consortium reminded me that it's more correct to use all lower case (non-capital) letters. Similarly, even though some HTML tags will work without a closing tag, closing tags should always be used so that your HTML code will be compatible with XML, a more advanced coding language I'll be discussing in a future book.

Web Safety

Creating a web site on the Internet is a fun-filled hobby which can help you make friends across the country or around the world. It's as safe as going for a walk in the park. But use the same care you would if you were in the park. You wouldn't give a stranger in the park your name, address, or phone number so don't put your name, address, or phone number on your web site.

The first rule of web safety is not to give out enough information on the Internet for someone to find you in your neighborhood.

Here's some tips to keep your new hobby a safe hobby:

- Use only your first name or use a nickname. It's much better to use "Steve" or "Skooter" than it is to use "Steve Williams". If you have an unusual name be sure to use a nickname even if you have to make one up yourself.

- Describe where you live in a very general way. For example, use "northern Idaho" instead of "Bonner's Ferry".

- Describe where you go to school in a very general way. Use "our junior high school" rather than "Cedar Rapids Junior High School".

- Don't use pictures that place you next to a local landmark which will reveal what neighborhood you live in.

- Use one of the web-based e-mail services described in Appendix C. You'll have the fun of making up your own e-mail address and it won't give a hint of who you are or where you live. It will also allow you to receive e-mail anywhere in the world when you go on vacation or if you move to a new city.

Now it's time to be creative and really have some fun!

Chapter 1
Your First Web Page

1.1 Introduction To HTML

HTML stands for HyperText Markup Language. "HyperText" means that information on one web page is connected to information on another web page by a link. Click on the link and your browser will take you to the connected web page. "Markup" means that plain unformatted text (ASCII text) has been marked up to show how it is to look when viewed in a web browser like Netscape Communicator or Internet Explorer.

> **Dave's Advice:** If I use a term you haven't heard before, like browser or ASCII, check the Glossary at the back of this book to find out what it means.

To understand how HTML code works, think of marking text with different color markers to indicate where you want the text to be shown in different ways such as bold, italic, or centered. The only difference is that with HTML instead of marking the text with colored markers you mark it with an "opening tag" at the beginning of the text and a "closing tag" at the end. The tags aren't visible when the file is viewed in a web browser.

HTML tags are easily recognized because they are enclosed in angled brackets. The opening tag gives the code for the format chosen, such as **<CENTER>**. The closing tag is the same except that it has a slash ("/") added between the first angled bracket and the code: **</CENTER>**. If you want to center a line on a page, for example, code it like this:

<CENTER>Welcome to Dave's Homepage!**</CENTER>**

Dave's Advice: Although some HTML tags will work without a closing tag, closing tags should always be used so that HTML code is compatible with XML, a more advanced Internet coding language.

1.2 Basic Web Page Setup

All HTML documents use the same basic page setup. Here's a step-by-step recipe:

1. Mark the web page with **<HTML>** at the very beginning and **</HTML>** at the very end to indicate that it's an HTML document.
2. Mark the header section of the page with **<HEAD>** and **</HEAD>**.
3. Mark the title of the page using **<TITLE>** and **</TITLE>** within the header section.

Dave's Advice: Choosing the right title for your web page is important. The title will appear on the top line of a visitor's browser when they view your page and it will be used by search engines to index your web page.

4. Mark the body section of the page using **<BODY>** and **</BODY>** right after the header section.
5. Now put it all together:
   <HTML>
   <HEAD>
   <TITLE>Type the title of your page here.**</TITLE>**
   </HEAD>
   <BODY>
   Type your page here.
   </BODY>
   </HTML>

1.3 Frequently-used HTML Tags

Now that you know the basic web page setup it's time to have a look at the HTML tags that you'll use most often.

- To center a word, a sentence, or a paragraph mark it with the tags **<CENTER>** and **</CENTER>**.

- To <u>underline</u> a word, a sentence, or a paragraph mark it with the tags **<U>** and **</U>**.

- To make a word, a sentence, or a paragraph "**bold**" mark it with the tags **<B>** and **</B>**.

- To print a word, a sentence, or a paragraph in "*italics*" mark it with the tags **<I>** and **</I>**.

- To "break" a line (to move to the left edge of the next line on the page) type **
**. It has the same effect as pressing the "Enter" key in a text editor. There is no closing tag.

- To begin a new paragraph (to move to the left edge of the next line on the page and then skip a line) surround the paragraph with the tags **<P>** and **</P>**.

> **Dave's Advice:** A quick way to center a paragraph is to add the attribute **ALIGN=CENTER** to the paragraph opening tag like this: **<P ALIGN=CENTER>**

- To add "a horizonal rule" (a line) to divide the page, type **<HR>**. There is no closing tag.

1.4 Nesting Tags

When combining two or more sets of HTML tags, the tags must be "nested" to work properly. Nesting means that one set of tags is placed between the other set of tags. There can't be an overlap. For example, these HTML tags are placed together correctly:
<B><I>Welcome to Dave's Homepage!**</I></B>**
while these HTML tags are not:
<B><I>Welcome to Dave's Homepage!**</B></I>**.

1.5 Spacing

To add vertical spacing between different parts of your page use several **
** tags. Using several **<P>** tags won't work. It will give you the same result as if you had used one **<P>** tag. The same rule applies for using the space bar to add several horizontal spaces in a row on a web page. It will give the same result as if you had used just one space.

> **Dave's Advice:** You can add multiple spaces to an HTML document by using the HTML code for a space ** **. For example, if you wish to indent the first line of a paragraph insert the code ** ** five times. (You can't use this code to line up several lines of text because HTML fonts are "proportional". Instead use tables described in Chapter 10.)

Now it's time to create your first web page. **Figure 1** shows our sample web page which you can use as a template. The HTML code is capitalized and bold. Don't change it. The text is just a sample. Change it so that it describes you or something which interests you. It might be about your best friend, your family, a hobby, a club you belong to, a sports team you're a member of, or your school. It will be your first homepage. It's the starting point for the rest of this book. Each chapter will show how to add one new feature to this basic web page.

1.6 Symbols

On our sample web page I used the HTML naming code **©** to place the copyright symbol (a "c" in a circle), with the year and my name at the bottom of the page. This code tells visitors to my web site that they may not use information or images from my web page without my permission.

Several symbols can be printed using naming codes (like **©**) or numerical codes (like **©**). Here are the codes for the symbols you are most likely to use:

©	= copyright symbol	= ©	= ©
&	= ampersand	= &	= &
"	= quotation mark	= "	= "
<	= less than	= <	= <
>	= greater than	= >	= >
	= non-breaking space	=	=

1.7 Naming Web Page Files

Save your file. You can name it anything you wish but it must end with either the file extension "htm" or the file extension "html" so that Internet browsers will recognize it as an HTML document. Some operating systems such as DOS allow only a three-character extension so if you're using DOS you'll have to

---

Figure 1

```
<HTML>
<HEAD>
<TITLE>Dave's Domain</TITLE>
</HEAD>
<BODY>
<CENTER>Welcome to Dave's Homepage!</CENTER>
<P>
Hi! My name is Dave.</P>
<P>
I'm fourteen years old and I live in Calgary, Alberta,
Canada.</P>
<P>
My home town is Canada's fifth largest city with a
population of 800,000. It's located on the Bow River where
the prairies meet the foothills of the Rocky Mountains. It's
the gateway to Banff National Park.</P>
<P>
Calgary is the oil and gas capital of Canada. It's surrounded
by grain farms and cattle ranches. The Winter Olympic
Games were held here in 1988. The World Police and Fire
Games were held here in 1997.</P>
<P>
Here are some things I'm interested in:</P>
<P>
<B>Music:</B> I've been playing guitar for three and a half
years. I play music by Eric Clapton, Metallica, and Jimi
Hendrix on my Fender Strat and my Gibson Les Paul. I'm in
a blues band and in a rock band. I like to listen to Kenny
Wayne Shepherd, Metallica, Collective Soul, and
Rammstein.</B>
<P>
<B>Books:</B> Brian Jacques is my favorite author. I also
enjoy books by Piers Anthony and Lloyd Alexander.</P>
<P>
<B>Sports:</B> I like biking in the summer, and
snowboarding in the winter. I played Little League Baseball
and I've tried basketball, soccer, fencing, and water-skiing.
</P>
<P>
<B>Hobbies:</B> I like playing games on the Internet,
computer programming, foosball, and paintball.</P>
```

Figure 1 (continued)

```
<P>
<B>School:</B> I'm in the ninth grade in junior high school.
I play guitar in the stage band.</P>
<P>
<B>Favorite Comics:</B> <I>Foxtrot</I> and <I>Calvin
and Hobbes</I>.</P>
<P>
<B>Favorite TV:</B> <I>X-Files</I>, <I>Frasier</I>, and
<I>King of the Hill</I>.</P>
<P>
<B>Favorite Movies:</B> <I>Men In Black </I>, <I>
Mission Impossible</I>, and <I>The Empire Strikes Back
</I>.</P>
<P>
<B>Heroes:</B> My heroes are Eric Clapton (the greatest
blues guitarist ever), John Carmack (creator of <I>Quake
</I>), and Linus Torvalds (creator of <I>Linux</I>).
<BR>
<BR>
<HR>
You can E-mail me at "dave@redwall.org".
<BR>
<BR>
&copy;1998 Dave
<BR></P>
</BODY>
</HTML>
```

use "htm". With Windows, Macs, Linux, or UNIX you can use either "htm" or "html".

I name my main web page "homepage.html" because the server I post my web pages on automatically searches for the homepage.html file. Most servers search for index.html. Some servers search for main.html. It all depends on how your Internet Service Provider (ISP) has set up its server. By using homepage.html I can give out a shorter address (known as a Uniform Resource Locator or URL) for my web site. Instead of giving my friends the URL "http://www.redwall.org/homepage.html" I give them "http://www.redwall.org" or even just "redwall.org".

1.8 Testing Web Pages

Now that you've created your first web page it's time to see how it looks through an Internet browser. Download and install the browser of your choice if you haven't already done so. (Appendix A shows where to obtain Netscape Communicator and Internet Explorer.)

1. Open your browser by double-clicking its icon.
2. Hold down the control key and type "O" for "open". The "Open Page" dialog box (Netscape) or the "Open" dialog box (Internet Explorer) will appear.
3. Type the drive, directory, and file name of your homepage.
   or
   Click the "Choose File" button (Netscape) or the "Browse" button (Internet Explorer) to locate and select your web page file.
4. Click the "Open" button (Netscape) or the "OK" button (Internet Explorer) and your browser will load your file. You'll see exactly how your web page will look on the Internet.
5. Check your page for typos and coding errors. Fix them and retest.

Dave's Advice: The most common HTML coding error is forgetting to type a closing tag for each opening tag. The second most common coding error is not "nesting" tags.

1.9 Publishing Web Pages

It's time to upload your web page file to an Internet web server. Appendix D shows where to get free web server space. Appendix A shows where to get the FTP program you'll use to upload the file. Appendix E explains how to use the FTP program. Appendix F will help you register your web site with the most popular search engines on the Internet so everyone can find it.

Connect to the Internet. Open your browser. Type in the URL of your web site and admire your new homepage. It should look something like what you see in **Figure 2**. You've now done all the hard work. The rest of this book will show you how to personalize your web site with all "the bells and whistles". That's the fun part of creating a web site. It's also the easy part.

Figure 2

Welcome to Dave's Homepage!

Hi! My name is Dave.

I'm fourteen years old and I live in Calgary, Alberta, Canada.

My home town is Canada's fifth largest city with a population of 800,000. It's located on the Bow River where the prairies meet the foothills of the Rocky Mountains. It's the gateway to Banff National Park.

Calgary is the oil and gas capital of Canada. It's surrounded by grain farms and cattle ranches. The Winter Olympic Games were held here in 1988. The World Police and Fire Games were held here in 1997.

Here are some things I'm interested in:

Music: I've been playing guitar for three and a half years. I play music by Eric Clapton, Metallica, and Jimi Hendrix on my Fender Strat and my Gibson Les Paul. I'm in a blues band and in a rock band. I like to listen to Kenny Wayne Shepherd, Metallica, Collective Soul, and Rammstein.

Books: Brian Jacques is my favorite author. I also enjoy books by Piers Anthony and Lloyd Alexander.

Sports: I like biking in the summer, and snowboarding in the winter. I played Little League Baseball and I've tried basketball, soccer, fencing, and water-skiing.

Hobbies: I like playing games on the Internet, computer programming, foosball, and paintball.

School: I'm in the ninth grade in junior high school. I play guitar in the stage band.

Favorite Comics: *Foxtrot* and *Calvin and Hobbes*.

Favorite TV: *X-Files*, *Frasier*, and *King of the Hill*.

Favorite Movies: *Men In Black*, *Mission Impossible*, and *The Empire Strikes Back*.

Heroes: My heroes are Eric Clapton (the greatest blues guitarist ever), John Carmack (creator of *Quake*), and Linus Torvalds (creator of *Linux*).

You can E-mail me at "dave@redwall.org".

©1998 Dave

3 1833 02363 980 7

Chapter 2
Headings And Lists

Now that you've got your web page up and running, the first challenge is to improve its layout. I mentioned spacing in Chapter 1.5 and I'll be covering tables in Chapter 10. Here I'll explain headings and lists, two easy-to-use layout tools.

2.1 Headings

The Heading tags **<H1>** and **</H1>** are used to make headings. They set the size of a line of text and make it bold just as if you had used the bold tags **<B>** and **</B>**. They also add an automatic paragraph break after the closing tag just as if you had inserted the paragraph tag **<P>** on the next line after the **</H1>** closing tag.

There are six HTML heading sizes: H1 is the largest; H6 is the smallest; and H4 is approximately the size of normal text. The tags used are **<H1>** and **</H1>** but with "1" changed to the size of the heading level you want to use, from 1 to 6. Heading tags can be used for a word, a line, a paragraph, or even a whole page. The HTML code looks like this:

<H2>Welcome to Dave's Homepage!**</H2>**

2.2 Lists

There are three common types of lists: ordered lists, unordered lists, and definition lists.

Ordered Lists

Ordered lists are lists where each line is numbered beginning with "1". Ordered lists use the tags <OL> and </OL> for the whole list and use the tags <LI> and</LI> for each "list item". The HTML code looks like this:

```
<OL>
<LI>chocolate</LI>
<LI>strawberry</LI>
<LI>vanilla</LI>
</OL>
```

When viewed in a browser the output of this code looks like this:

1 chocolate
2 strawberry
3 vanilla

> **Dave's Advice:** You can choose the type of numbers to be used in the list by adding the **TYPE** attribute to the <OL> opening tag like this: **<OL TYPE="1">**
> where "1" will give arabic numerals, "i" will give lower case Roman numerals, "I" will give upper case Roman numerals, "a" will give lower case letters of the alphabet, and "A" will give upper case letters of the alphabet.

Unordered Lists

Unordered lists are lists which have a bullet (a filled circle that looks like a bullet coming at you) at the beginning of each line. Unordered lists use the tags <UL> and </UL> for the whole list and use the tags <LI> and</LI> for each "list item". The HTML code looks like this:

```
<UL>
<LI>blue</LI>
<LI>green</LI>
<LI>red</LI>
</UL>
```

In a browser the output of this code looks like this:

• blue
• green
• red

> **Dave's Advice:** You can change the appearance of a bullet by adding the **TYPE** attribute to the **\<UL\>** opening tag like this: **\<UL TYPE="DISC"\>**
> where **DISC** will give a filled circle, **CIRCLE** will give an unfilled circle, and **SQUARE** will give an unfilled square.

Definition Lists

Definition lists are usually used for dictionary lists (glossaries). They're made up of two parts: a term (a word) and its definition. The term is shown at the left margin and the definition is given on the next line, indented from the left margin. Definition lists use the tags **\<DL\>** and **\</DL\>** with the term being surrounded by the tags **\<DT\>** and **\</DT\>** and the definition being surrounded by the tags **\<DD\>** and **\</DD\>**. The HTML code looks like this:

```
<DL>
<DT>FTP</DT>
<DD>File Transfer Protocol</DD>
<DT>HTML</DT>
<DD>Hypertext Markup Language</DD>
<DT>pixel</DT>
<DD>picture element</DD>
</DL>
```

When viewed in a browser the output of this code looks like this:

FTP
    File Transfer Protocol
HTML
    HyperText Markup Language
pixel
    picture element

Figure 3 shows the HTML code for our sample homepage with a heading, an ordered list, and an unordered list added. **Figure 4** shows how the page looks when viewed through an Internet browser.

Figure 3

```
<HTML>
<HEAD>
<TITLE>Dave's Domain</TITLE>
</HEAD>
<BODY>
<CENTER><H1>Welcome to Dave's Homepage!</H1>
</CENTER>
<P>
Hi! My name is Dave.</P>
<P>
I'm fourteen years old and I live in Calgary, Alberta,
Canada.</P>
<P>
My home town is Canada's fifth largest city with a
population of 800,000. It's located on the Bow River where
the prairies meet the foothills of the Rocky Mountains. It's
the gateway to Banff National Park.</P>
<P>
Calgary is the oil and gas capital of Canada. It's surrounded
by grain farms and cattle ranches. The Winter Olympic
Games were held here in 1988. The World Police and Fire
Games were held here in 1997.</P>
<P>
Here are some things I'm interested in:</P>
<P>
<B>Music:</B> I've been playing guitar for three and a half
years. I play music by Eric Clapton, Metallica, and Jimi
Hendrix on my Fender Strat and my Gibson Les Paul. I'm in
a blues band and in a rock band. I like to listen to
<OL>
<LI>Kenny Wayne Shepherd</LI>
<LI>Metallica</LI>
<LI>Collective Soul</LI>
<LI>Rammstein</LI>
</OL></P>
<P>
<B>Books:</B> Brian Jacques is my favorite author. I also
enjoy books by Piers Anthony and Lloyd Alexander.</P>
```

Figure 3 (continued)

```
<P>
<B>Sports:</B> I like biking in the summer, and
snowboarding in the winter. I played Little League Baseball
and I've tried
<UL>
<LI>basketball</LI>
<LI>soccer</LI>
<LI>fencing</LI>
<LI>water-skiing</LI>
</UL></P>

<P>
<B>Hobbies:</B> I like playing games on the Internet,
computer programming, foosball, and paintball.</P>

<P>
<B>School:</B> I'm in the ninth grade in junior high school.
I play guitar in the stage band.</P>

<P>
<B>Favorite Comics:</B> <I>Foxtrot</I> and <I>Calvin
and Hobbes</I>.</P>

<P>
<B>Favorite TV:</B> <I>X-Files</I>, <I>Frasier</I>, and
<I>King of the Hill</I>.</P>

<P>
<B>Favorite Movies:</B> <I>Men In Black </I>, <I>
Mission Impossible</I>, and <I>The Empire Strikes Back
</I>.</P>

<P>
<B>Heroes:</B> My heroes are Eric Clapton (the greatest
blues guitarist ever), John Carmack (creator of <I>Quake
</I>), and Linus Torvalds (creator of <I>Linux</I>).

<BR>
<BR>
<HR>
You can e-mail me at "dave@redwall.org".
<BR>
<BR>
&copy;1998 Dave
<BR></P>

</BODY>
</HTML>
```

Figure 4

Welcome to Dave's Homepage!

Hi! My name is Dave.

I'm fourteen years old and I live in Calgary, Alberta, Canada.

My home town is Canada's fifth largest city with a population of 800,000. It's located on the Bow River where the prairies meet the foothills of the Rocky Mountains. It's the gateway to Banff National Park.

Calgary is the oil and gas capital of Canada. It's surrounded by grain farms and cattle ranches. The Winter Olympic Games were held here in 1988. The World Police and Fire Games were held here in 1997.

Here are some things I'm interested in:

Music: I've been playing guitar for three and a half years. I play music by Eric Clapton, Metallica, and Jimi Hendrix on my Fender Strat and my Gibson Les Paul. I'm in a blues band and in a rock band. I like to listen to

1. Kenny Wayne Shepherd
2. Metallica
3. Collective Soul
4. Rammstein

Books: Brian Jacques is my favorite author. I also enjoy books by Piers Anthony and Lloyd Alexander.

Sports: I like biking in the summer, and snowboarding in the winter. I played Little League Baseball and I've tried

- basketball
- soccer
- fencing
- water-skiing

Hobbies: I like playing games on the Internet, computer programming, foosball, and paintball.

School: I'm in the ninth grade in junior high school. I play guitar in the stage band.

Favorite Comics: *Foxtrot* and *Calvin and Hobbes*.

Favorite TV: *X-Files*, *Frasier*, and *King of the Hill*.

Favorite Movies: *Men In Black*, *Mission Impossible*, and *The Empire Strikes Back*.

Figure 4 (continued)

Heroes: My heroes are Eric Clapton (the greatest blues guitarist ever), John Carmack (creator of *Quake*), and Linus Torvalds (creator of *Linux*).

You can E-mail me at "dave@redwall.org".
©1998 Dave

Chapter 3
Hyperlinks

3.1 Introduction To Hyperlinks

If you've been surfing the 'net for awhile you're already familiar with hyperlinks. They're the images or underlined words which when clicked on take you to another place on the web page you're on or to another web page altogether. Hyperlinks can link to any file on the Internet including image files and sound files.

To create a hyperlink, use the HTML tags **<A>** and **</A>** to anchor the source web page to the target web page like this:

<A HREF="the location of the target web page">a description of the target web page**</A>**

The opening tag **<A>** is modified by the attribute **HREF**, the hypertext reference, which uses a Uniform Resource Locator (URL) to show where the target file can be found. (URLs are explained in the next section.) Then a word or phrase is given to describe the web page or the information given in the web page. This description is followed by the closing tag **</A>**. For example, here's a hyperlink to Brian Jacques' homepage:

<A HREF="http://www.redwall.org/dave/jacques.html">The Official Brian Jacques Homepage</A>

> **Dave's Advice:** The most common mistake made when creating a hyperlink is forgetting the second quotation mark (just before the >).

3.2 Uniform Resource Locators

A Uniform Resource Locator (URL) is the Internet address of a file. It's made up of a protocol, a domain name, a directory name, and a file name. Here are the four parts which make up the URL for The Official Brian Jacques Homepage:

http: //www.redwall.org   /dave/   jacques.html

The protocol is a set of rules which decide how computers communicate. Think of it as a language like French or Spanish. HTTP stands for HyperText Transfer Protocol, the most common protocol on the world wide web. It's used to transfer a file from the server it's stored on to the browser on your computer. Another common protocol, the File Transfer Protocol (FTP), is used to download files from the server they're stored on to your computer's hard drive, or to upload web page files from your computer's hard drive to the web server.

The domain name is the address of the web server on which the file is stored. In this case, The Redwall Club has its own domain name: "www" stands for world wide web, "redwall" stands for The Redwall Club, and "org" stands for organization.

The remainder of the URL names the "dave" directory and the "jacques.html" file which the hyperlink is targeting.

> **Dave's Advice:** Though HTML is not case sensitive (capital letters vs. non-capital letters), URLs are. It's important when setting up hyperlinks that you enter the URL using upper case (capital letters) and lower case (non-capital letters) correctly.

URLs: Absolute Address vs Relative Address

If the source web page file and the target file are in the same directory on the web server, it isn't necessary to give the complete URL of the target file in a hyperlink. Only the file name is needed. If the source web page file and the target file are on the same server but aren't in the same directory, it's possible to use a shortcut which gives the location of the target file relative to the web page file. This type of file address is called a "relative address". I don't recommend using relative addresses. I think there's less chance of making a mistake using "absolute addresses" (complete URLs).

3.3 Basic Hyperlinks

A basic hyperlink, the one described in the introduction to this chapter, connects one web page to another web page. The HTML code looks like this:

<A HREF="the URL of the target web page">a description of the target web page**</A>**

For example, the following basic hyperlink takes you to Redwall Abbey, Brian Jacques' web site:

<A HREF="http://www.redwall.org/homepage.html"> Redwall Abbey**</A>**

> **Dave's Advice:** "/homepage.html" can be omitted from the above URL and the hyperlink will still find the target file because The Redwall Club server automatically searches for "homepage.html" as the default file.

The HTML code and the URL won't show up on the web page when it's viewed in a browser. The words "Redwall Abbey" will be underlined and will be shown in color, either a color you specify for hyperlinks as described in Chapter 4.4 or the default color set by the visitor's browser.

> **Dave's Advice:** You can remove the underline from a single hyperlink by adding the attribute
> **STYLE="text-decoration: none" CLASS="Link"**
> to the **<A>** tag like this:
> **<A STYLE="text-decoration: none" CLASS="Link" HREF="http://www.redwall.org">**Redwall Abbey**</A>**
> or you can remove the underlines from all hyperlinks on a web page by adding the code
> **<STYLE>A {text-decoration: none}</STYLE>**
> to the header of the web page. See **Figures 13 and 14** on pages 61-65 to see what our sample web page looks like with the underlines removed from all hyperlinks.

3.4 Internal Hyperlinks

An internal hyperlink connects one place on a web page to another place on the same web page. It's most often used to set up a Table of Contents for a long web page. (A group of internal hyperlinks at the top of the page connects to each section of the page.) Internal hyperlinks are also used on Frequently Asked Questions web pages to link questions and answers.

The first step in adding internal hyperlinks to a web page is to assign a name to each section of the web page using the **NAME** attribute with the anchor tag, **<A>**:

<A NAME="the name assigned to that section"></A>
For example we could use **<A NAME="Comics"></A>** to code the "Favorite Comics" section of our sample web page. The Table of Contents would include a hyperlink to the Favorite Comics section which would look like this:

<A HREF="#Comics">Favorite Comics</A>
where "#" tells the Internet browser that the name "Comics" has been assigned to a section of our web page.

In **Figure 5** we have added HTML tags to our web page for a simple Table of Contents. **Figure 6** shows how this web page appears on the 'net.

3.5 Combined Hyperlinks

The two types of hyperlinks just described can be combined to direct a visitor to a specific section of another of your web pages. It's also possible to direct visitors to specific sections of other authors' web pages if they have assigned names to the sections of their web pages. For example, the hyperlink **<A HREF="http://www.redwall.org/dave/davepage.html #Comics">Dave's Favorite Comics</A>**
will take you to the Favorite Comics section of our web page.

3.6 E-mail Hyperlinks

When an e-mail hyperlink is clicked, the visitor's Internet browser loads a pre-addressed e-mail form which the visitor can use to send an e-mail message to the e-mail address specified. Usually this will be your e-mail address, but it can be any e-mail address you specify. Visitors can send the e-mail while they're viewing your HTML document. They don't need to open a separate e-mail program. The HTML code for an e-mail hyperlink looks like this:

<A HREF="MAILTO:e-mail address">the name of the person at that e-mail address</A>
where "e-mail address" is the address to which the e-mail is to be sent. You can specify the subject line in the e-mail by adding

Figure 5

```
<HTML>
<HEAD>
<TITLE>Dave's Domain</TITLE>
</HEAD>

<BODY>
<A NAME="Top"></A>
<CENTER><H1>Welcome to Dave's Homepage!</H1>
</CENTER>

<P>
Hi! My name is Dave.</P>

<P>
I'm fourteen years old and I live in Calgary, Alberta,
Canada.</P>

<P>
My home town is Canada's fifth largest city with a
population of 800,000. It's located on the Bow River where
the prairies meet the foothills of the Rocky Mountains. It's
the gateway to Banff National Park.</P>

<P>
Calgary is the oil and gas capital of Canada. It's surrounded
by grain farms and cattle ranches. The Winter Olympic
Games were held here in 1988. The World Police and Fire
Games were held here in 1997.</P>

<P>
Here are some things I'm interested in:</P>

<P>
<B>Music:</B> I've been playing guitar for three and a half
years. I play music by Eric Clapton, Metallica, and Jimi
Hendrix on my Fender Strat and my Gibson Les Paul. I'm
in a blues band and in a rock band. I like to listen to
<OL>
<LI>Kenny Wayne Shepherd</LI>
<LI>Metallica</LI>
<LI>Collective Soul</LI>
<LI>Rammstein</LI>
</OL></P>

<P>
<A NAME="Middle"></A>
<B>Books:</B> Brian Jacques is my favorite author. I also
enjoy books by Piers Anthony and Lloyd Alexander.</P>
```

Figure 5 (continued)

```
<P>
<B>Sports:</B> I like biking in the summer, and
snowboarding in the winter. I played Little League Baseball
and I've tried
<UL>
<LI>basketball</LI>
<LI>soccer</LI>
<LI>fencing</LI>
<LI>water-skiing</LI>
</UL></P>
<P>
<A NAME="Bottom"></A>
<B>Hobbies:</B> I like playing games on the Internet,
computer programming, foosball, and paintball.</P>
<P>
<B>School:</B> I'm in the ninth grade in junior high school.
I play guitar in the stage band.</P>
<P>
<B>Favorite Comics:</B> <I>Foxtrot</I> and <I>Calvin
and Hobbes</I>.</P>
<P>
<B>Favorite TV:</B> <I>X-Files</I>, <I>Frasier</I>, and
<I>King of the Hill</I>.</P>
<P>
<B>Favorite Movies:</B> <I>Men In Black</I>, <I>
Mission Impossible</I>, and <I>The Empire Strikes Back
</I>.</P>
<P>
<B>Heroes:</B> My heroes are Eric Clapton (the greatest
blues guitarist ever), John Carmack (creator of <I>Quake
</I>), and Linus Torvalds (creator of <I>Linux</I>).
<BR>
<BR>
<CENTER>| <A HREF="#Top"> Top of the Page</A>
| <A HREF="#Middle"> Middle of the Page</A>
| <A HREF="#Bottom"> Bottom of the Page</A> |
</CENTER>
<HR>
You can e-mail me at "dave@redwall.org".<BR>
<BR>
&copy;1998 Dave
<BR></P>
</BODY>
</HTML>
```

Figure 6

Welcome to Dave's Homepage!

Hi! My name is Dave.

I'm fourteen years old and I live in Calgary, Alberta, Canada.

My home town is Canada's fifth largest city with a population of 800,000. It's located on the Bow River where the prairies meet the foothills of the Rocky Mountains. It's the gateway to Banff National Park.

Calgary is the oil and gas capital of Canada. It's surrounded by grain farms and cattle ranches. The Winter Olympic Games were held here in 1988. The World Police and Fire Games were held here in 1997.

Here are some things I'm interested in:

Music: I've been playing guitar for three and a half years. I play music by Eric Clapton, Metallica, and Jimi Hendrix on my Fender Strat and my Gibson Les Paul. I'm in a blues band and in a rock band. I like to listen to

1. Kenny Wayne Shepherd
2. Metallica
3. Collective Soul
4. Rammstein

Books: Brian Jacques is my favorite author. I also enjoy books by Piers Anthony and Lloyd Alexander.

Sports: I like biking in the summer, and snowboarding in the winter. I played Little League Baseball and I've tried

- basketball
- soccer
- fencing
- water-skiing

Hobbies: I like playing games on the Internet, computer programming, foosball, and paintball.

School: I'm in the ninth grade in junior high school. I play guitar in the stage band.

Favorite Comics: *Foxtrot* and *Calvin and Hobbes*.

Favorite TV: *X-Files*, *Frasier*, and *King of the Hill*.

Favorite Movies: *Men In Black*, *Mission Impossible*, and *The Empire Strikes Back*.

Figure 6 (continued)

Heroes: My heroes are Eric Clapton (the greatest blues guitarist ever), John Carmack (creator of *Quake*), and Linus Torvalds (creator of *Linux*).

| Top of the Page | Middle of the Page | Bottom of the Page |

You can E-mail me at "dave@redwall.org".

©1998 Dave

PAGE 24   HYPERLINKS

the code "**?subject=your choice of subject**" to the link, like so:
HREF="MAILTO:webmaster@redwall.org?subject=
Dave's Quick 'n' Easy Web Pages">E-mail Dave Lindsay**</A>**

Setting the subject line is especially useful if you're using an e-mail autoresponder to answer your e-mail with messages which differ depending on the subject of the incoming e-mail.

Figure 7 shows the source document for our basic web page (without the Table of Contents coded in **Figures 5 and 6**), with some basic hyperlinks and a mail hyperlink added to it. **Figure 8** shows how this web page looks on the 'net.

3.7 Image Hyperlinks

I'll be explaining in detail how to use images on your web page in Chapter 5. Here I'll show how an image may be used in place of text to describe a target web page and act as a hyperlink.

An image hyperlink connects to a target web page when clicked, in exactly the same way a text hyperlink does. Here's the HTML code needed:
<A HREF="the URL of the target web page"><IMG SRC= "the URL of an image which describes the target web page"></A>
where **IMG SRC** stands for "image source". For example, the following HTML code uses a painting of Redwall Abbey saved as a file named "ABBEY.gif" as a hyperlink to the Redwall Abbey web site:
<A HREF="http://www.redwall.org"><IMG SRC= "http:// www.redwall.org/images/ABBEY.gif"></A>

Images are often used for e-mail hyperlinks with everything from buttons, to envelopes, to animated letters jumping into mailboxes being used. Here is the HTML code for one of the mail button hyperlinks I use
<A HREF="MAILTO:webmaster@redwall.org"><IMG SRC= "http://www.redwall.org/images/Email.gif"></A>
You can see it in use in **Figure 12** on page 53.

> **Dave's Advice:** An image hyperlink is normally surrounded by a colored border two pixels wide. This border can be eliminated by setting its thickness to zero withthe attribute **BORDER**:
> **<A HREF="MAILTO:dave@redwall.org"><IMG SRC= "http://www.redwall.org/images/Email.gif" BORDER="0"></A>**

Figure 7

```
<HTML>
<HEAD>
<TITLE>Dave's Domain</TITLE>
</HEAD>

<BODY>

<CENTER><H1>Welcome to Dave's Homepage!</H1>
</CENTER>

<P>
Hi! My name is Dave.</P>

<P>
I'm fourteen years old and I live in <A HREF="http://www.
visitor.calgary.ab.ca/">Calgary</A>, Alberta, Canada.</P>

<P>
My home town is Canada's fifth largest city with a
population of 800,000. It's located on the Bow River where
the prairies meet the foothills of the Rocky Mountains. It's
the gateway to <A HREF="http://www.canadianrockies
.net">Banff National Park</A>.</P>

<P>
Calgary is the oil and gas capital of Canada. It's surrounded
by grain farms and cattle ranches. The Winter Olympic
Games were held here in 1988. The World Police and Fire
Games were held here in 1997.</P>

<P>
Here are some things I'm interested in:</P>

<P>
<B>Music:</B> I've been playing guitar for three and a half
years. I play music by <A HREF="http://www.fgi.net/
~dbwatty/eric.htm">Eric Clapton</A>, <A HREF="http://
www.metallica.com/">Metallica</A>, and <A HREF=
"http://www.jimi-hendrix.com/">Jimi Hendrix</A> on my
<A HREF="http://www.fender.com/electricguitars/strats/
americanseries/amerstrat.html">Fender Strat</A> and my
<A HREF="http://www.gibson.com/products/epiphone/
inst/Les-Paul/ENST.html">Gibson Les Paul</A>. I'm in a
blues band and in a rock band. I like to listen to
<OL>
<LI><A HREF="http://www.kwsband.com/">Kenny Wayne
Shepherd</A></LI>
<LI><A HREF="http://www.metallica.com/">Metallica
</A></LI>
```

Figure 7 (continued)

```
<LI><A HREF="http://www.csoul.com">Collective Soul
</A></LI>
<LI><A HREF="http://www.rammstein.de">Rammstein
</A></LI>
</OL></P>

<P>
<B>Books:</B> <A HREF="http://www.redwall.org/dave/
jacques.html">Brian Jacques</A> is my favorite author. I
also enjoy books by <A HREF="http://www.hipiers.
com">Piers Anthony</A> and <A HREF="http://www.
friend.ly.net/scoop/biographies/alexanderlloyd/index
.html">Lloyd Alexander</A>.</P>

<P>
<B>Sports:</B> I like biking in the summer, and snow-
boarding in the winter. I played Little League Baseball and
I've tried
<UL>
<LI>basketball</LI>
<LI>soccer</LI>
<LI>fencing</LI>
<LI>water-skiing</LI>
</UL></P>

<P>
<B>Hobbies:</B> I like playing games on the Internet,
computer programming, <A HREF="http://www.foosball.
com/">foosball </A>, and <A HREF="http://www.capture
theflag.com/">paintball </A>.</P>

<P>
<B>School:</B> I'm in the ninth grade in junior high school.
I play guitar in the stage band.</P>

<P>
<B>Favorite Comics:</B> <A HREF="http://www.
foxtrot.com"><I>Foxtrot</I></A> and <A HREF="http://
www.calvinandhobbes.com"><I>Calvin and Hobbes</I>
</A>.</P>

<P>
<B>Favorite TV:</B> <A HREF="http://www.theX-
Files.com/"><I>X-Files</I></A>, <A HREF="http://
www.paramount.com/television/frasier/"><I>Frasier
</I></A>, and <A HREF= "http://www.fox.com/king
ofthehill/index.html"><I>King of the Hill</I></A>.</P>
```

Figure 7 (continued)

```
<P>
<B>Favorite Movies:</B> <A HREF="http://www.
meninblack.com/main.html"><I>Men In Black </I></A>,
<A HREF="http://www.missionimpossible.com/"><I>
Mission Impossible</I></A>, and <A HREF="http://www.
starwars.com/episode-v/"> <I>The Empire Strikes Back
</I></A>.</P>

<P>
<B>Heroes:</B> My heroes are <A HREF="http://www
.fgi.net/~dbwatty/eric.htm">Eric Clapton</A> (the greatest
blues guitarist ever), <A HREF="http://www.idsoftware
.com/corporate/idhist.html">John Carmack</A> (creator of
<I>Quake</I>), and <A HREF="http://www.bootnet.com/
youaskedforit/lip_linux_manifesto.html">Linus Torvalds
</A> (creator of <I>Linux</I>).

<BR>
<BR>
<HR>
You can <A HREF="MAILTO:dave@redwall.org">e-mail
</A> me.
<BR>
<BR>
&copy;1998 Dave
<BR></P>

</BODY>
</HTML>
```

Figure 8

Welcome to Dave's Homepage!

Hi! My name is Dave.

I'm fourteen years old and I live in <u>Calgary</u>, Alberta, Canada.

My home town is Canada's fifth largest city with a population of 800,000. It's located on the Bow River where the prairies meet the foothills of the Rocky Mountains. It's the gateway to <u>Banff National Park</u>.

Calgary is the oil and gas capital of Canada. It's surrounded by grain farms and cattle ranches. The Winter Olympic Games were held here in 1988. The World Police and Fire Games were held here in 1997.

Here are some things I'm interested in:

Music: I've been playing guitar for three and a half years. I play music by <u>Eric Clapton</u>, <u>Metallica</u>, and <u>Jimi Hendrix</u> on my <u>Fender Strat</u> and my <u>Gibson Les Paul</u>. I'm in a blues band and in a rock band. I like to listen to

1. <u>Kenny Wayne Shepherd</u>
2. <u>Metallica</u>
3. <u>Collective Soul</u>
4. <u>Rammstein</u>

Books: <u>Brian Jacques</u> is my favorite author. I also enjoy books by <u>Piers Anthony</u> and <u>Lloyd Alexander</u>.

Sports: I like biking in the summer, and snowboarding in the winter. I played Little League Baseball and I've tried

- basketball
- soccer
- fencing
- water-skiing

Hobbies: I like playing games on the Internet, computer programming, <u>foosball</u>, and <u>paintball</u>.

School: I'm in the ninth grade in junior high school. I play guitar in the stage band.

Favorite Comics: *Foxtrot* and *Calvin and Hobbes*.

Favorite TV: *X-Files*, *Frasier*, and *King of the Hill*.

Favorite Movies: *Men In Black*, *Mission Impossible*, and *The Empire Strikes Back*.

Figure 8 (continued)

Heroes: My heroes are <u>Eric Clapton</u> (the greatest blues guitarist ever), <u>John Carmack</u> (creator of *Quake*), and <u>Linus Torvalds</u> (creator of *Linux*).

You can <u>E-mail</u> me.

©1998 Dave

Chapter 4
Color

4.1 Introduction To Web Page Color

The most dramatic change you can make to your web page is to add color. You can color the background, text, hyperlinks, and tables (which are explained in Chapter 10).

Web Safe Colors

Web page colors often appear differently when viewed on different computers. This color variance isn't usually a problem for personal web pages where using a particular shade of color isn't essential, but it can make text more difficult to read. The situation arises because many computers on the Internet are capable of producing only 256 colors, or even just 16 colors. These computers create the additional colors needed for a web page by presenting different colored pixels blended together in a pattern to approximate the color specified. (This process is called "dithering".) To further complicate things, different platforms (Windows, Macintosh, UNIX) and different browsers (Netscape, Internet Explorer) use different color palettes. When these palettes don't include a specified color, the color is dithered. Fortunately there are 216 non-dithering web safe colors which are common to Netscape and Internet Explorer on both Windows and Macintosh (but not UNIX) platforms. Web authors can control how their web page colors appear on the majority of Internet computers by using these 216 colors.

Specifying Colors

Internet browsers can recognize many colors by name. Unfortunately, different browsers don't match the same names to the same colors. Where Netscape assigns a shiny metallic color to the name "gold", Internet Explorer gives it a flat orange yellow color. A more exact way to specify colors uses hexadecimal color codes instead of color names. These codes are made up of seven characters in the format "#rrggbb". The "rr" digits set how much of the color is red; the "gg" digits set how much of the color is green; and the "bb" digits set how much of the color is blue. Hexadecimal codes are based on sixteen numbers instead of the ten we use in the decimal system. Since there isn't a single digit to represent each of the numbers from 10 to 15 the hexadecimal system uses the letters A, B, C, D, E, F for these numbers.

Several helpful web sites provide hexadecimal color codes in a way that makes it easy to choose colors which work well together for background, text, and links:

Webmaster's Color Laboratory
http://www.visibone.com/colorlab/

All You Need To Know About Web Safe Colors
http://www.webdevelopersjournal.com/articles/websafe1/websafe_colors.html

Web Safe Colors Chart
http://www.nedcomm.nm.org/doc/webcolor.htm

Netscape Color Names
http://ccwf.cc.utexas.edu/~kiele/WebDesign/colors.html

Color Center
http://www.hidaho.com/colorcenter/

Color Picker For HTML
http://www.asahi-net.or.jp/~FX6M-FJMY/java09e.html

Search Topics: Web Safe Colors
                 HTML Color

> **Dave's Advice:** The world wide web is constantly changing. Web sites move to new servers; new web sites are set up; and old web sites are closed down. When I suggest web sites to visit, I'll also provide a "Search Topic". That way if a web site I've suggested is no longer at the URL I've given, you can use a search engine (see Appendix F) to search for the topic listed and locate either the site I've recommended or one just like it.

4.2 Background Color

To color your web page background (in this case "black") add the attribute **BGCOLOR** to the opening **<BODY>** tag like this:
<BODY BGCOLOR="#000000">

4.3 Text Color

It's possible to color text for an entire web page, or for just a word or two (or just a paragraph or two).

To color the text of an entire web page (in this case "tan") add the attribute **TEXT** to the opening **<BODY>** tag this way:
<BODY TEXT="#D2B48C">
When you color both the text and the background of your web page , the opening **<BODY>** tag looks like this:
<BODY BGCOLOR="#000000" TEXT="#D2B48C">

To color text for just a word or two,or just a paragraph or two, (in this case "lightskyblue") use the attribute **COLOR** with the tags **<FONT>** and **</FONT>** like this:
<FONT COLOR="#87CEFA">Welcome to Dave's Page!
</FONT>

> **Dave's Advice:** Text color set with the **<FONT>** tag takes precedence over text color set with the **<BODY>** tag. This feature allows you to assign color for your text with the **<BODY>** tag and then assign a different color for your paragraph headings with the **<FONT>** tag.

4.4 Hyperlink Color

To set the color of hyperlinks, add the attributes **LINK** (in this case "aquamarine") and **VLINK** (in this case "lightseagreen") to the opening **<BODY>** tag like this:
<BODY LINK="#7FFFD4" VLINK="#20B2AA">

---

where **LINK** is a hyperlink which hasn't been visited yet and **VLINK** is a "visited link", a hyperlink which the viewer has already visited. When you color background, text, and hyperlinks the opening <BODY> tag looks like this:

<BODY BGCOLOR="#000000" TEXT="#D2B48C" LINK="#7FFFD4" VLINK="#20B2AA">

4.5 Table Color

I'll show how to use tables on your web page in Chapter 10. Here I'll explain how to color table backgrounds and table borders.

Table Cell Color

To color the backgrounds of table cells, add the attribute **BGCOLOR** to the tag <TABLE>, <TR>, or <TD> like this:

<TABLE BGCOLOR="red">

if you wish the background color of the whole table to be red.

<TR BGCOLOR="green">

if you wish the background color for a table row to be green.

<TD BGCOLOR="blue">

if you wish the background color for a single table cell to be blue.

Table cell colors take precedence over table row colors, and table row colors take precedence over whole table colors.

> **Dave's Advice:** It's not possible to color the background of an empty table cell. You must use the the naming code for a blank space ( ) as the content of an empty cell if you wish to color its background.

Table Border Color

To color a table border, add the attribute **BORDERCOLOR** to the <TABLE> tag like this:

<TABLE BORDERCOLOR="blue">

When you color both the table background and the table border the <TABLE> tag looks like this:

<TABLE BGCOLOR="green" BORDERCOLOR="blue">

Now it's time to add some color to your web page! **Figure 9** shows the source document for our sample web page with color added. **Figure 10** shows a screen print of this web page as seen in Netscape.

Figure 9

```
<HTML>
<HEAD>
<TITLE>Dave's Domain</TITLE>
</HEAD>

<BODY BGCOLOR="#000000" TEXT="#D2B48C" LINK=
"#7FFFD4" VLINK="#20B2AA">


<CENTER><H1><FONT COLOR="#87CEFA">Welcome to
Dave's Homepage!</FONT></H1></CENTER>

<P>
Hi! My name is Dave.</P>

<P>
I'm fourteen years old and I live in <A HREF="http://www.
visitor.calgary.ab.ca/">Calgary</A>, Alberta, Canada.</P>

<P>
My home town is Canada's fifth largest city with a
population of 800,000. It's located on the Bow River where
the prairies meet the foothills of the Rocky Mountains. It's
the gateway to <A HREF="http://www.canadianrockies
.net">Banff National Park</A>.</P>

<P>
Calgary is the oil and gas capital of Canada. It's surrounded
by grain farms and cattle ranches. The Winter Olympic
Games were held here in 1988. The World Police and Fire
Games were held here in 1997.</P>

<P>
Here are some things I'm interested in:</P>

<P>
<B><FONT COLOR="#87CEFA">Music:</FONT></B> I've
been playing guitar for three and a half years. I play music
by <A HREF="http://www.fgi.net/~dbwatty/eric.htm">Eric
Clapton</A>, <A HREF="http://www.metallica.com">
Metallica</A>, and <A HREF="http://www.jimi-hendrix
.com">Jimi Hendrix</A> on my <A HREF="http://www
.fender.com/electricguitars/strats/americanseries
/amerstrat.html">Fender Strat</A> and my <A HREF
="http://www.gibson.com/products/epiphone/inst/Les-
Paul/ENST.html">Gibson Les Paul</A>. I'm in a blues band
and in a rock band. I like to listen to
```

Figure 9 (continued)

```
<OL>
<LI><A    HREF="http://www.kwsband.com">Kenny
Wayne Shepherd</A></LI>
<LI><A HREF="http://www.metallica.com">Metallica
</A></LI>
<LI><A HREF="http://www.csoul.com">Collective Soul
</A></LI>
<LI><A HREF="http://www.rammstein.de">Rammstein
</A></LI>
</OL></P>

<P>
<B><FONT COLOR="#87CEFA">Books:</FONT></B>
<A HREF="http://www.redwall.org/dave/jacques.html">
Brian Jacques</A> is my favorite author. I also enjoy books
by <A HREF="http://www.hipiers.com">Piers Anthony
</A> and <A HREF="http://www.friend.ly.net/scoop/
biographies/alexanderlloyd/index.html">Lloyd
Alexander</A>.</P>

<P>
<B><FONT COLOR="#87CEFA">Sports:</FONT></B> I
like biking in the summer, and snowboarding in the winter.
I played Little League Baseball and I've tried
<UL>
<LI>basketball</LI>
<LI>soccer</LI>
<LI>fencing</LI>
<LI>water-skiing</LI>
</UL></P>

<P>
<B><FONT COLOR="#87CEFA">Hobbies:</FONT></B> I
like playing games on the Internet, computer programming,
<A HREF="http://www.foosball.com/">foosball</A>, and
<A HREF="http://www.capturetheflag.com/">paintball
</A>.</P>

<P>
<B><FONT COLOR="#87CEFA">School:</FONT></B> I'm
in the ninth grade in junior high school. I play guitar in the
stage band.</P>

<P>
<B><FONT   COLOR="#87CEFA">Favorite  Comics:
</FONT></B> <A HREF="http://www.foxtrot.com"><I>
Foxtrot</I></A> and <A HREF="http://www.calvinand
hobbes.com"><I>Calvin and Hobbes</I></A>.</P>
```

Figure 9 (continued)

```
<P>
<B><FONT COLOR="#87CEFA">Favorite TV:</FONT>
</B> <A HREF="http://www.theX-Files.com/"><I>X-Files
</I></A>, <A HREF="http://www.paramount.com/
television/frasier/"><I>Frasier</I></A>, and <A HREF
="http://www.fox.com/kingofthehill/index
.html"><I>King of the Hill</I></A>.</P>

<P>
<B><FONT COLOR="#87CEFA">Favorite Movies:</FONT>
</B> <A HREF="http://www.meninblack.com/main.html">
<I>Men In Black</I></A>, <A HREF="http://www
.missionimpossible.com/"><I>Mission Impossible</I></A>,
and <A HREF="http://www.starwars.com/episode-v/">
<I>The Empire Strikes Back</I></A>.</P>

<P>
<B><FONT COLOR="#87CEFA">Heroes:</FONT></B>
My heroes are <A HREF="http://www.fgi.net/~db
watty/eric.htm">Eric Clapton</A> (the greatest blues
guitarist ever), <A HREF="http://www.idsoftware.com/
corporate/idhist.html">John Carmack</A> (creator of
<I>Quake</I>), and <A HREF="http://www.bootnet.com/
youaskedforit/lip_linux_manifesto.html">Linus Torvalds
</A> (creator of <I>Linux</I>).
<BR>
<BR>
<HR>
You can <A HREF="MAILTO:dave@redwall.org">e-mail
</A> me.
<BR>
<BR>
&copy;1998 Dave
<BR></P>

</BODY>
</HTML>
```

Figure 10

Welcome to Dave's Homepage!

Hi! My name is Dave.

I'm fourteen years old and I live in Calgary, Alberta, Canada.

My home town is Canada's fifth largest city with a population of 800,000. It's located on the Bow River where the prairies meet the foothills of the Rocky Mountains. It's the gateway to Banff National Park.

Calgary is the oil and gas capital of Canada. It's surrounded by grain farms and cattle ranches. The Winter Olympic Games were held here in 1988. The World Police and Fire Games were held here in 1997.

Here are some things I'm interested in:

Music: I've been playing guitar for three and a half years. I play music by Eric Clapton, Metallica, and Jimi Hendrix on my Fender Strat and my Gibson Les Paul. I'm in a blues band and in a rock band. I like to listen to

1 Kenny Wayne Shepherd

Document Done

Chapter 5
Images

5.1 Introduction To Internet Images

Images are an extension of color. Adding them to your web page can bring it to life.

Image Formats

Two image formats are commonly used on the Internet: Joint Photographic Experts Group (JPEG) and Graphic Interchange Format (GIF). You can tell which format an image is in from its file extension. JPEG file names end in ".jpeg" or ".jpg" while GIF file names end in ".gif".

JPEG is best for color photographs and other high-quality images such as "art gallery" quality paintings because it can handle thousands of colors.

GIF is best for cartoons and drawings because it's limited to just 256 colors. It's also the right choice for images which include text because it doesn't blur the edges of text the way JPEG does. GIF images can also have transparent backgrounds (Chapter 5.7) and can be animated (Chapter 8).

There are two types of GIF image: interlaced and non-interlaced. Interlaced images load in horizonal stripes, with the quality of the image improving as the image loads. Non-interlaced images load row-by-row from the top down, with final quality being provided from the start. Interlaced images appear to load faster than non-interlaced images because a fuzzy image appears almost immediately and becomes clearer as it's being watched.

Image Format Conversion

Dave's Advice: Most image editing programs work in a similar way. In the examples in this book I use Paint Shop Pro because it can do everything you need to do with images to prepare them for the Internet, and it's affordable. Best of all, you can download it immediately and try it free for thirty days. See Appendix A to find out how.

To convert an image to GIF or JPEG from another format:
1. open the image file in Paint Shop Pro
2. choose "Save As" from the "File" menu
3. choose the directory you wish to save the file in
4. type in the name you wish to give the file
5. click on the "Save As Type:" drop-down menu
6. choose either "Compuserve Graphics Interchange (*.gif)" or "JPEG -JFIF Compliant (*.jpg, *.jif, *.jpeg)"
7. for GIF images click on the "Options" button.
   a. click on "Version 89a"
   b. click on either "Interlaced" or "Non-interlaced"
   c. click on the "OK" button
8. click on the "Save" button

Dave's Advice: If you want to edit an image and save it as JPEG or GIF, it's best to do the editing while the image is in bitmap (".bmp") format or Paint Shop Pro (".psp") format, and then convert the image to JPEG or GIF. If you convert your image to JPEG and then edit it, the quality of the image will degrade each time you save the file because of the compression formula JPEG uses. If you convert your image to GIF first and then edit it, you won't be able to use all the image editing tools because many of them require 24 bit color, and GIF is 8 bit color.

5.2 Adding Images To Web Pages

To add an image to your web page, upload the image file to your ISP's web server. (Appendix E explains how.) Then insert the <IMG> (image) opening tag on your page where the image is to be placed. Add the **SRC** (source) attribute to the <IMG> tag to indicate which image file is to be used and where it's located. When the file is located in the same directory on the web server as the web page, only the image file name is needed. The HTML code looks like this:

<IMG SRC="rainbow.gif">

Otherwise, a complete URL for the image file is given, like this:

<IMG SRC="http://www.redwall.org/images/rainbow.gif">
<IMG> doesn't have a closing tag.

> **Dave's Advice:** Visitors to your web site will have different size monitors set at different resolutions. To control how your web page looks on different monitors you can set the width of divider images (like the rainbow-colored divider above) as a percentage of the width of the screen this way:
> <IMG SRC="http://www.redwall.org/images/rainbow.gif" WIDTH="75%">

Some visitors to your web site won't be able to view images. Some will have text-only browsers. Some will have graphics mode disabled on their browser so that web pages load faster. Some will be blind people using a text-reader Internet browser. You can make your web page user-friendly for everyone by adding the attribute **ALT** to your <IMG> tag like this:

<IMG SRC="image.gif" ALT="description">

where **ALT** stands for alternate and "description" describes either the image or the image link depending on how the image is being used. Here are two examples:

<IMG SRC="jacques.jpg" ALT="photograph of Brian Jacques">

and

<IMG SRC="ABBEY.gif" ALT="link to Redwall Abbey Homepage">

5.3 Image Alignment

You can center an image horizontally on your web page using the tags <CENTER> and </CENTER>:

<CENTER><IMG SRC="ABBEY.gif"></CENTER>

or you can align an image with either the left margin or the right margin of the page by adding the **ALIGN** attribute to the **IMG** tag and setting it equal to "right" or "left":

<IMG SRC="ABBEY.gif" ALIGN="right">

The **ALIGN** attribute can also be used with the choices "top", "middle", or "bottom" to set the vertical placement of an image within a single line of text:

I give this book a **<IMG SRC="fivestar.gif" ALIGN= "bottom">** rating.

It's a little more tricky to set the vertical spacing of text placed beside an image. For now, use the **ALIGN** attribute to place the image to the left or to the right, then use the **
** tag to set the vertical spacing of text beside the image. This is not an ideal solution as your web page will look different when viewed through different size monitors. A better answer is provided by Tables described in Chapter 10.

> **Dave's Advice:** To place a caption (a title) beside an image, and have the next line of text after the caption begin below the image, use **<BR CLEAR="all">** to end the caption.

5.4 Image Spacing

You can set the amount of space around an image by modifying the **IMG** tag with the attributes **HSPACE** (horizonal space) and **VSPACE** (vertical space). The HTML code looks like this:

<IMG SRC="ABBEY.gif" HSPACE="25" VSPACE="20">

where the space is measured in pixels. The quickest way to learn how to use these spacing attributes is to experiment with different settings on your web page.

5.5 Picture Frames

You can place a "picture frame" around an image by using a table border. (Tables are explained in Chapter 10.) Just create a one-celled table, with your image as the content, and with a border as it's frame. The HTML code looks like this:

<TABLE BORDER="10" BORDERCOLOR="gold">
<TR><TD><IMG SRC="ABBEY.gif"></TD></TR>
</TABLE>

where border width is measured in pixels. To see picture frames in use, visit The Redwall Gallery at: http://www.redwall.org/redwall/gallery.html

---

5.6 Quicker Image Loading

When images are added to a web page, the web page takes much longer to load into an Internet browser than it previously did because image files are very large compared with HTML files. It's possible to quicken image loading by reducing the size of the image file. This can be done by shrinking the size of the image and/or by reducing the number of colors used in the image.

Shrinking An Image
To shrink the size of an image:
1. Open the image in Paint Shop Pro.
2. Choose "Resize" from the "Image" menu.
3. Click on "Resize All Layers" and "Maintain Aspect Ratio of...".
4. Click on either "Pixel Size" or "Percentage of Original".
5. Type in the size you want for either "Width" or "Height" (but not both or you'll distort your image).
6. Click "OK".
7. Choose "Save As" from the "File" menu and save your re-sized image.

Reducing The Number Colors In An Image
To reduce the number of colors used in an image:
1. Open the image in Paint Shop Pro.
2. Choose "Count Colors" from the "Colors" menu to find out how many colors your image currently uses. Then click "OK".
3. Choose "Decrease Color Depth" from the "Colors" menu.
4. Click on "X Colors (4/8 bit)".
5. Type in the number of colors you would like to use.
6. Click "OK".
7. If you don't like the way the new image looks, choose "Undo Decrease Colors to X" from the "Edit" menu and try again.
8. Once you're happy with the result, choose "Save As" from the "File" menu and save your new image.

Modifying HTML Code
When an Internet browser loads an image, it calculates the size of the image as it loads. If the size of the image is specified in the HTML code, the browser doesn't have to make this calclulation, and the image loads faster.

To learn the size of an image, open it in Paint Shop Pro and place the mouse cursor over it. The size of the image will be shown on the right side of the task bar. This size can then be specified on the web page using the **HEIGHT** and **WIDTH** attributes with the **<IMG>** tag:

<IMG SRC="image.gif" HEIGHT="h" WIDTH="w">

where "h" is the height of the image in pixels and "w" is the width of the image in pixels. For example:

<IMG SRC="rainbow.gif" HEIGHT="5" WIDTH="576">

Thumbnail Images

Another way to quicken web page loading when a web page includes a large image is to use a "thumbnail" image. It's a small version of the image (usually about 75 pixels wide by 75 pixels high) which is placed on the web page in place of the original image. It's made into an "image hyperlink" (Chapter 3.7) which links to the original image when clicked. The web page can load faster but can still provide a larger version of the image for visitors who are interested.

5.7 Transparent Image Backgrounds

An image can be made to appear as if it was drawn directly on a web page by making the image background transparent. This modification is easy to accomplish but works only on GIF images. Three situations can be encountered:

1. The image background is a single color and that color is not used in the image.
2. The image background is a single color and that color is used in the image.
3. The image background is made up of several colors, a pattern, or objects which are to be eliminated.

Single-color Background, Color Not Used In Image

If the background of an image is a single color which is not being used in the image itself, here's what to do:

1. Open the image in Paint Shop Pro.
2. Choose the "Dropper" tool.
3. Position the Dropper tool over the background.
4. Click the right mouse button to load the background color into the Color Palette as the background color.
5. Open the "Colors" menu and choose "Set Palette Transparency".
6. Click "Set the transparency value to the current

background color".

7. Click "Proof" which will show you what the image looks like with the transparency color you've selected.
8. If you're not happy with the result click "Cancel" and start again at number "2" above.
9. If you're happy with the result click on "OK".
10. Choose "Save As" from the "File" menu.
11. Click the "Save As Type:" drop-down menu.
12. Choose "Compuserve Graphics Interchange (*.gif)".
13. Click the "Options" button.
14. Click "Version 89a" and either "Interlaced" or "Non-interlaced".
15. Click the "OK" button and then the "Save" button.

Single-color Background, Color Used In Image

If the background of an image is a single color which is being used in the image itself, the background color will have to be changed to another color before it can be made transparent. Otherwise parts of the image itself will also appear transparent. Here's what to do:

1. Open the image in Paint Shop Pro.
2. Click the "Color Palette" icon (the icon with vertical color bars, located just below the "Selections" menu on the upper tool bar) to display the Color Palette on the right side of the monitor screen.
3. Choose the "Dropper" tool and move it over the color palette to select a color.
4. Pick a bright color like pink which is easy to see and is not being used in the image itself.
5. Click the right mouse button to load that color into the Color Palette as the background color.

Dave's Advice: If you have difficulty loading the new color as the background color, it's probably because your image is not set to handle enough colors. You can fix this problem by choosing "Increase Color Depth" from the "Colors" menu and selecting "16 million colors (24 bit)". When you go to set the transparency value, Paint Shop Pro will remind you to reduce the color depth back to 256 colors and the necessary menu will pop up.

6. Choose the "Flood Fill" tool (it's the tool that looks like a can of house paint tipping over), move the mouse over

the background, and click the right mouse button to change the background color.

7. Go to number "5." in the section on "Single-color Background, Color Not Used In Image" on page 44.

Multi-colored Background

If the background of an image is made up of several colors or contains a pattern or other objects, it will have to be changed to a single color which is not being used in the image itself before it can be made transparent.

1. Open the image in Paint Shop Pro.
2. Click the "Color Palette" icon (the icon with vertical color bars, located just below the "Selections" menu on the upper tool bar) to display the Color Palette on the right side of the monitor screen.
3. Choose the "Dropper" tool and move it over the color palette to select a color.
4. Pick a bright color like pink which is easy to see and is not being used in the image itself.
5. Click the right mouse button to load that color into the Color Palette as the background color. (If you encounter a problem refer to "Dave's Advice" on page 45.)
6. Choose the "Flood Fill" tool (it's the tool that looks like a can of house paint tipping over), move the mouse over the background, and click the right mouse button to change the background color. Move it over each large area which needs to have the color changed and click the right mouse button.
7. Choose the "Paintbrushes" tool and paint the smaller areas by hand.

Dave's Advice: It's easier to paint the smaller areas by hand if you zoom in on the area you want to paint.

To zoom in on the area you want to paint, choose the "Zoom" tool (it's the tool that looks like a magnifying glass), place the mouse cursor over the area of the image you want to work on, and click the left mouse button to zoom in. Click again until you have the image enlarged as much as you'd like. (To zoom out, click the right mouse button.)

Dave's Advice: It's easier to paint the smaller areas by hand if you shrink the size of the paintbrush tip.

To shrink the size of the paintbrush tip, choose the "Paint Brushes" tool, click on the "Control Palette" icon (the icon to the left of the Color Palette icon, just below the "Selections" menu on the upper tool bar), and click the "Brush Tip" tab. Then choose the size and shape of the brush you'd like to use.

8. Once the background is a single color, go to number "5." in the section on "Single-color Background, Color Not Used In Image" on page 44.

5.8 Obtaining Images

Web page images are available from several sources for free. They can be downloaded from image libraries on the Internet. They can be downloaded directly from other web pages on the Internet. They can be scanned from books or drawings. Or they can be drawn directly to an image file with a program like Windows Paint, Mac Paint, or Paint Shop Pro.

Online Image Libraries

The first images you're likely to add to your web page are icons, buttons, dividers, and bullets. You can download these types of images from online image libraries for free. Here are the URLs of some popular online image libraries:

Clipart Castle
http://www.clipartcastle.com/

Jelane's Free Web Graphics
http://www.erinet.com/jelane/families/

Image-O-rama
http://members.aol.com/dcreelma/imagesite/image.htm

Cheryl's Image Gallery
http://www.artbycheryl.com/

Webshots
http://www.webshots.com/homepage.html

Search Topics: Free Web Images
                  Free Image Libraries
                  Free Web Clip Art

Downloading Images Directly From Web Pages

To download an image directly from the Internet, place your mouse cursor over the image and click your right mouse button. Then click "Save Image As" in the menu which appears. Specify which directory you want to save the image file in, and choose a name for your file. Click the "Save" button.

> **Dave's Advice:** Always ask permission to use images you find on the web. Then download the images, and upload them to your own web server. **Never link your web page to an image file on someone else's web server!** Doing so slows down their server and limits the number of visitors to their site. If their ISP charges for bandwidth (the amount of data down-loaded) it will also cost them money.

Scanning Images

Scanners are quite inexpensive now (my flat bed cost just $45.) but if you don't own one, you can probably use one at your school or public library. Here's how to scan photographs or artwork yourself: Install your scanner and open Paint Shop Pro. From the "File" menu choose "Import", then "TWAIN", and then "Acquire". Adjust the scanner settings to match the picture you are about to scan.

> **Dave's Advice:** I recommend scanning at 75 dots per inch (dpi). Image quality on a monitor won't improve at a dpi much greater than that. A higher resolution will only result in a bigger image file which will take longer to load.

Scan your photographs or drawings following the instructions which came with your scanner. If you're happy with the results choose "Save As" from the "File" menu and save your image file. If you're not happy with the results click on "Rescan" and start again.

I've added an image, an image divider, and an image hyper-link to our sample web page. Check out **Figure 11** for the HTML code and **Figure 12** for a screen print of the finished web page.

Figure 11

```
<HTML>
<HEAD>
<TITLE>Dave's Domain</TITLE>
</HEAD>

<BODY BGCOLOR="#000000" TEXT="#D2B48C" LINK=
"#7FFFD4" VLINK="#20B2AA">

<CENTER><H1><FONT COLOR="#87CEFA">Welcome to
Dave's Homepage!</FONT></H1></CENTER>

<IMG SRC="http://www.redwall.org/images/Dave.jpg"
WIDTH="137" HEIGHT="170" ALIGN="left" HSPACE=
"25" VSPACE="25" ALT="Photograph of Dave">
<BR>
<BR>
<BR>

<P>
Hi! My name is Dave.</P>

<P>
I'm fourteen years old and I live in <A HREF="http://www.
visitor.calgary.ab.ca/">Calgary</A>, Alberta, Canada.</P>
<BR>
<BR>
<BR>
<BR>
<BR>
<BR>
<BR>

<P>
My home town is Canada's fifth largest city with a
population of 800,000. It's located on the Bow River where
the prairies meet the foothills of the Rocky Mountains. It's
the gateway to <A HREF="http://www.canadianrockies
.net">Banff National Park</A>.</P>
```

Figure 11 (continued)

<P>
Calgary is the oil and gas capital of Canada. It's surrounded by grain farms and cattle ranches. The Winter Olympic Games were held here in 1988. The World Police and Fire Games were held here in 1997.</P>

<P>
Here are some things I'm interested in:</P>

<P>
<B><FONT COLOR="#87CEFA">Music:</FONT></B> I've been playing guitar for three and a half years. I play music by <A HREF="http://www.fgi.net/~dbwatty/eric.htm">Eric Clapton</A>, <A HREF="http://www.metallica.com"> Metallica</A>, and <A HREF="http://www.jimi-hendrix .com">Jimi Hendrix</A> on my <A HREF="http://www .fender.com/electricguitars/strats/americanseries /amerstrat.html">Fender Strat</A> and my <A HREF ="http://www.gibson.com/products/epiphone/inst/Les-Paul/ENST.html">Gibson Les Paul</A>. I'm in a blues band and in a rock band. I like to listen to
<OL>
<LI><A   HREF="http://www.kwsband.com">Kenny Wayne Shepherd</A></LI>
<LI><A HREF="http://www.metallica.com">Metallica </A></LI>
<LI><A HREF="http://www.csoul.com">Collective Soul </A></LI>
<LI><A HREF="http://www.rammstein.de">Rammstein </A></LI>
</OL></P>

<P>
<B><FONT COLOR="#87CEFA">Books:</FONT></B> <A HREF="http://www.redwall.org/dave/jacques.html"> Brian Jacques</A> is my favorite author. I also enjoy books by <A HREF="http://www.hipiers.com">Piers Anthony </A> and <A HREF="http://www.friend.ly.net/scoop/ biographies/alexanderlloyd/index.html">Lloyd Alexander</A>.</P>

Figure 11 (continued)

```
<P>
<B><FONT COLOR="#87CEFA">Sports:</FONT></B> I
like biking in the summer, and snowboarding in the winter.
I played Little League Baseball and I've tried
<UL>
<LI>basketball</LI>
<LI>soccer</LI>
<LI>fencing</LI>
<LI>water-skiing</LI>
</UL></P>


<P>
<B><FONT COLOR="#87CEFA">Hobbies:</FONT></B> I
like playing games on the Internet, computer programming,
<A HREF="http://www.foosball.com/">foosball</A>, and
<A HREF="http://www.capturetheflag.com/">paintball
</A>.</P>


<P>
<B><FONT COLOR="#87CEFA">School:</FONT></B> I'm
in the ninth grade in junior high school. I play guitar in the
stage band.</P>


<P>
<B><FONT  COLOR="#87CEFA">Favorite  Comics:
</FONT></B> <A HREF="http://www.foxtrot.com"><I>
Foxtrot</I></A> and <A HREF="http://www.calvinand
hobbes.com"><I>Calvin and Hobbes</I></A>.</P>


<P>
<B><FONT COLOR="#87CEFA">Favorite TV:</FONT>
</B> <A HREF="http://www.theX-Files.com/"><I>X-Files
</I></A>,  <A  HREF="http://www.paramount.com/
television/frasier/"><I>Frasier</I></A>, and <A HREF
="http://www.fox.com/kingofthehill/index
.html"><I>King of the Hill</I></A>.</P>


<P>
<B><FONT COLOR="#87CEFA">Favorite Movies:</FONT>
</B> <A HREF="http://www.meninblack.com/main.html">
<I>Men In Black </I></A>, <A HREF="http://www
.missionimpossible.com/"><I>Mission Impossible</I></A>,
```

Figure 11 (continued)

```
and <A HREF="http://www.starwars.com/episode-v/">
<I>The Empire Strikes Back</I></A>.</P>


<P>
<B><FONT COLOR="#87CEFA">Heroes:</FONT></B>
My heroes are <A HREF="http://www.fgi.net/~db
watty/eric.htm">Eric Clapton</A> (the greatest blues
guitarist ever), <A HREF="http://www.idsoftware.com/
corporate/idhist.html">John Carmack</A> (creator of
<I>Quake</I>), and <A HREF="http://www.bootnet.com/
youaskedforit/lip_linux_manifesto.html">Linus Torvalds
</A> (creator of <I>Linux</I>).
<BR>
<BR>
<CENTER>
<IMG SRC="http://www.redwall.org/images/rainbow.gif"
WIDTH="85%" HEIGHT="1" ALT="Rainbow-colored
divider"></CENTER>
<BR>
<A HREF="MAILTO:dave@redwall.org"><IMG SRC=
"http://www.redwall.org/images/Email.gif" WIDTH="68"
HEIGHT="32" ALIGN="left" BORDER="0" ALT="E-mail
Hyperlink"></A>
<BR>
<BR>
&copy;1998 Dave
<BR></P>


</BODY>
</HTML>
```

Figure 12

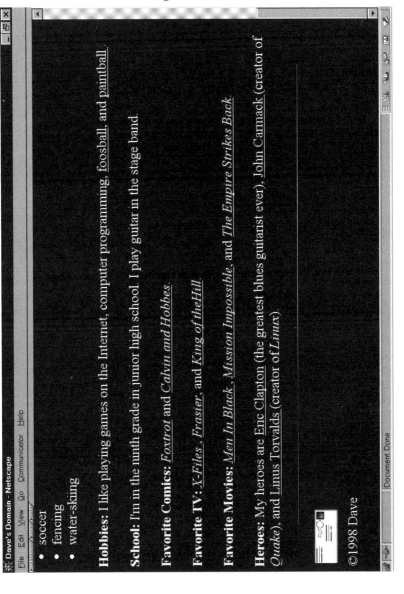

Chapter 6
Background Images

6.1 Introduction To Background Images

Adding a background image to your web page can create atmosphere. On the Redwall Abbey web site I use a background which looks like parchment. It adds a medieval atmosphere to match the medieval theme of the *Redwall* adventures.

Though any GIF or JPEG image can be used as a web page background, some images work better than others. Too large an image will take too long to load. Most images used for backgrounds are only about 160 pixels wide by 160 pixels high. Browsers "tile" (repeat) these small images many times to fill the screen. An image can't be too "busy" either, or it will make web page content difficult to read. And an image must have a "soft" edge so that it looks like a smooth surface rather than a series of rectangles when it's tiled across the screen .

6.2 Adding Background Images To Web Pages

Once you've found a suitable image, you can install it as a background image on your web page by uploading it to your

web server and adding the **BACKGROUND** attribute to the
<BODY> opening tag:
<BODY BACKGROUND="image.gif">

Here's the opening **<BODY>** tag for our sample web page:
**<BODY BGCOLOR="#000000" TEXT="#D2B48C"LINK=
"#7FFFD4" VLINK="#20B2AA" BACKGROUND="http://
www.redwall.org/images/blackmagic.gif">**

> **Dave's Advice:** When you use a background image on your
> web page, set the background color of the web page the
> same as the main color in the background image. A visitor
> will then see the background color while the background
> image is loading, and will be able to begin reading the web
> page right away. If for any reason the background image
> can't load, the visitor will still see the background color you
> intended.

6.3 Adding Background Images To Tables

Adding background images to tables is not considered
"accepted HTML practice", but it works. Here's how to add
background images to table cells using the **BACKGROUND**
attribute with the table tags **<TABLE>**, **<TR>**, and **<TD>**:
<TABLE BACKGROUND="image.gif">
to use an image as a background for a whole table,
<TR BACKGROUND="image.gif">
to use an image as a background for a table row, or
<TD BACKGROUND="image.gif">
to use an image as a background for a table cell.

> **Dave's Advice:** It's not possible to add a background image
> to an empty table cell. You must use the the naming code
> for a blank space ** ** as the content of an empty cell if
> you wish to add a background image.

I'll be covering the use of tables in detail in Chapter 10.

6.4 Downloading Background Images

The easiest way to obtain a background image for your web
page is to download it from one of the many free online image
libraries:
Julianne's Background Textures:
http://www.sfsu.edu/~jtolson/textures/textures.htm

Absolute Background Textures Archive
http://www.grsites.com/textures/

Realm Graphics
http://www.ender-design.com/rg/backidx.html

Winderosa
http://www.winderosa.com/backgrounddirectory.html

Baylor Background Images
http://www.baylor.edu/textures/

Search Topic: Free Web Backgrounds

It's also possible to download a background image directly from a web page, in the same way you download a regular image directly from a web page. The process and 'netiquette described in Chapter 5.8 are the same.

6.5 Creating Background Images

If you want an original-looking web page you'll want to create your own background image. You can scan in different materials such as paper, cloth, wood, rock, plants, or even your dad's old diploma. Then modify the image to suit your page. You can also use a draw or paint program to design something really unique. Here are a few tips to help you design an effective background image:

1. Keep your image small, about 160 pixels by 160 pixels.
2. Adjust the brightness and contrast to fade the image so that your web page content will be easy to read against the background.
3. Use the "unsharp filter" or the "smooth" tool of your paint program around the edges of the image to ensure that your background is seamless when the image is tiled.

Detailed tips and advice on creating background images are available from:

Lori's Web Graphics: Creating Backgrounds
http://loriweb.pair.com/bg.html

Image Lessons - Creating Background Images
http://baus.hypermart.net/img9.html

Scream Design - Photoshop Tips
http://www.screamdesign.com/graphics/photoshop/tips/index.html

Search Topic: Create Background Images

Chapter 7
Message Banners

7.1 Introduction To Message Banners

A good way to make your web page more interesting is to add movement, and the easiest way to add movement is to add a Message Banner. A Message Banner is a text message which scrolls across a web page. It can be placed in the Status Bar at the bottom of the browser or it can be placed in a Form Field anywhere on the web page. Message Banners can be set to run automatically or they can be set to run only when clicked. The second kind gives a visitor the choice of whether to activate the banner or not, making the web page interactive.

The code for a Message Banner is written in JavaScript, and is placed between the HTML tags **<SCRIPT>** and **</SCRIPT>** in the Header of the web page right after the Title. JavaScript is more finicky than HTML so you must type the code exactly as shown. JavaScript uses brackets, both the regular kind ( ) which you find above the "9" and the "0", and the curly kind { } which you find to the right of the "P" on your keyboard. Don't mix them up. They perform different functions.

7.2 Message Banners In The Status Bar

The Message Banner which is easiest to add to your web page is the one which places the message in the Status Bar at the bottom of your browser window. Just add the following JavaSript code to the Header section of your web page right after the Title:

```
<SCRIPT LANGUAGE="JavaScript">
<!--
var delayAA=150;
var messageAA="Type your message here.";
var timerAA=0;
var alignRightAA=0;
while (alignRightAA++<120) messageAA=" "+messageAA;
function BannerAA( )
{window.status=messageAA.substring(timerAA++,messageAA.length);
if (timerAA==messageAA.length) timerAA=0;
setTimeout ("BannerAA( )",delayAA);}
BannerAA( );
//-->
</SCRIPT>
```

Replace "Type your message here." with the message you want on your web page. Be sure to include the quotation marks around it. It can be a short message or it can be a long message made up of several sentences.

Experiment with the settings for speed and spacing by changing the number "**150**" in "**var delay=150**" and the number "**120**" in "**(alignRight++<120)**" to get the banner just right for your web page.

7.3 Message Banners In Form Fields

Placing a Message Banner in a Form Field allows you to place your message anywhere on your web page so that the message matches the text and images nearby.

First place this JavaScript code in the Header section of your Web Page right after the Title:

```
<SCRIPT LANGUAGE="JavaScript">
<!--
var delayBB=150;
var messageBB="Type your message here.";
var timerBB=0;
var alignRightBB=0;
while (alignRightBB++<60) messageBB=" "+messageBB;
function BannerBB( )
{document.bannerBB.bannerField.value=messageBB.substring
(timerBB++,messageBB.length);
if (timerBB==messageBB.length) timerBB=0;
setTimeout ("BannerBB( )",delayBB);}
//-->
</SCRIPT>
```

> **Dave's Advice:** It's important that the code:
> **{document.banner.bannerField.value=message.substring (timer++,message.length);**
> is typed all together, but it's okay if your text editor wraps it on to two lines as mine has.

Second add the attribute **onLoad="BannerBB( )"** to the **<BODY>** opening tag of your web page like this:
<BODY onLoad="BannerBB( )">

Third use the HTML tags **<FORM>** and **</FORM>** to create a Form Field on your web page where you'd like to place your message, like this:
<FORM NAME="bannerBB">
<INPUT TYPE="text" NAME="bannerField" SIZE=60>
</FORM>

You can change the size of the Form Field by changing the "**60**" in both **SIZE=60** between the HTML tags **<FORM>** and **</FORM>** and in "**(alignRight++<60)**" in the JavaScript code. You can change the speed of the message by changing the number "**150**" in "**var delay=150**" in the JavaScript code.

7.4 Clickable Message Banners In Form Fields

A Clickable Message Banner can make your web page interactive by giving visitors the choice of whether to access your message or not.

First place this JavaScript code in the Header section of your Web Page right after the Title:

```
<SCRIPT LANGUAGE="JavaScript">
<!--
var delayCC=150;
var messageCC="Type your message here.";
var timerCC=0;
var alignRightCC=0;
while (alignRightCC++<60) messageCC=" "+messageCC;
function BannerCC( )
{document.bannerCC.bannerField.value=messageCC.substring
(timerCC++,messageCC.length);
if (timerCC==messageCC.length) timerCC=0;
setTimeout ("BannerCC( )",delayCC);}
//-->
</SCRIPT>
```

Dave's Advice on the previous page applies here too.

Second use the HTML tags **<FORM>** and **</FORM>** to create a Form Field on your web page where you'd like to place your message, like this:

```
<FORM NAME="bannerCC">
<INPUT TYPE="text" NAME="bannerField" SIZE=60
VALUE="Click here to start the message." onFocus=
"{BannerCC( )}">
</FORM>
```

Replace the message "Click here to start the message" with something more appropriate for your web page.

You can change the size of the Form Field by changing the "**60**" in both **SIZE=60** between the HTML tags **<FORM>** and **</FORM>** and in "**(alignRight++<60)**" in the JavaScript code. You can change the speed of the message by changing the number "**150**" in "**var delay=150**" in the JavaScript code.

A clickable Message Banner has been added to a Form Field in our sample web page. The code is given in **Figure 13** and a screen print of the finished web page is shown in **Figure 14.**

Figure 13

```
<HTML>
<HEAD>
<TITLE>Dave's Domain</TITLE>
<SCRIPT LANGUAGE="JavaScript">
<!--

var delayCC=150;
var messageCC="My home town is Canada's fifth largest
city with a population of 800,000.    It's located on the Bow
River where the prairies meet the foothills of the Rocky
Mountains.    It's the gateway to Banff National Park.
Calgary is the oil and gas capital of Canada.    It's
surrounded by grain farms and cattle ranches.    The
Winter Olympic Games were held here in 1988.    The
World Police and Fire Games were held here in 1997.";
var timerCC=0;
var alignRightCC=0;
while (alignRightCC++<45) messageCC=" "+messageCC;
function BannerCC( )
{document.bannerCC.bannerField.value=messageCC.substring
(timerCC++,messageCC.length);
if (timerCC==messageCC.length) timerCC=0;
setTimeout ("BannerCC( )",delayCC);}
//-->
</SCRIPT>
<STYLE>A {text-decoration: none}</STYLE>
</HEAD>


<BODY BGCOLOR="#000000" TEXT="#D2B48C" LINK=
"#7FFFD4" VLINK="#20B2AA" BACKGROUND="http://
www.redwall.org/images/blkmagic.gif">


<CENTER><H1><FONT COLOR="#87CEFA">Welcome to
Dave's Homepage!</FONT></H1></CENTER>


<IMG SRC="http://www.redwall.org/images/Dave.jpg"
WIDTH="137" HEIGHT="170" ALIGN="left" HSPACE=
"25" VSPACE="25" ALT="Photograph of Dave">
<BR>
<BR>
<BR>
```

Figure 13 (continued)

```
<P>
Hi! My name is Dave.</P>


<P>
I'm fourteen years old and I live in <A HREF="http://www.
visitor.calgary.ab.ca/">Calgary</A>, Alberta, Canada.</P>
<BR>


<FORM NAME="bannerCC">
<INPUT TYPE="text" NAME="bannerField" SIZE=45
VALUE="Click here to learn more about my home town."
onFocus="{BannerCC( )}">
</FORM>
<BR>
<BR>
<BR>


<P>
Here are some things I'm interested in:</P>


<P>
<B><FONT COLOR="#87CEFA">Music:</FONT></B> I've
been playing guitar for three and a half years. I play music
by <A HREF="http://www.fgi.net/~dbwatty/eric.htm">Eric
Clapton</A>, <A HREF="http://www.metallica.com">
Metallica</A>, and <A HREF="http://www.jimi-hendrix
.com">Jimi Hendrix</A> on my <A HREF="http://www
.fender.com/electricguitars/strats/americanseries
/amerstrat.html">Fender Strat</A> and my <A HREF
="http://www.gibson.com/products/epiphone/inst/Les-
Paul/ENST.html">Gibson Les Paul</A>. I'm in a blues band
and in a rock band. I like to listen to
<OL>
<LI><A    HREF="http://www.kwsband.com">Kenny
Wayne Shepherd</A></LI>
<LI><A HREF="http://www.metallica.com">Metallica
</A></LI>
<LI><A HREF="http://www.csoul.com">Collective Soul
</A></LI>
<LI><A HREF="http://www.rammstein.de">Rammstein
</A></LI>
</OL></P>
```

Figure 13 (continued)

```
<P>
<B><FONT COLOR="#87CEFA">Books:</FONT></B>
<A HREF="http://www.redwall.org/dave/jacques.html">
Brian Jacques</A> is my favorite author. I also enjoy books
by <A HREF="http://www.hipiers.com">Piers Anthony
</A> and <A HREF="http://www.friend.ly.net/scoop/
biographies/alexanderlloyd/index.html">Lloyd
Alexander</A>.</P>


<P>
<B><FONT COLOR="#87CEFA">Sports:</FONT></B> I
like biking in the summer, and snowboarding in the winter.
I played Little League Baseball and I've tried
<UL>
<LI>basketball</LI>
<LI>soccer</LI>
<LI>fencing</LI>
<LI>water-skiing</LI>
</UL></P>


<P>
<B><FONT COLOR="#87CEFA">Hobbies:</FONT></B> I
like playing games on the Internet, computer programming,
<A HREF="http://www.foosball.com/">foosball</A>, and
<A HREF="http://www.capturetheflag.com/">paintball
</A>.</P>


<P>
<B><FONT COLOR="#87CEFA">School:</FONT></B> I'm
in the ninth grade in junior high school. I play guitar in the
stage band.</P>


<P>
<B><FONT    COLOR="#87CEFA">Favorite    Comics:
</FONT></B> <A HREF="http://www.foxtrot.com"><I>
Foxtrot</I></A> and <A HREF="http://www.calvinand
hobbes.com"><I>Calvin and Hobbes</I></A>.</P>


<P>
<B><FONT COLOR="#87CEFA">Favorite TV:</FONT>
</B> <A HREF="http://www.theX-Files.com/"><I>X-Files
</I></A>,  <A   HREF="http://www.paramount.com/
```

Figure 13 (continued)

television/frasier/"><I>Frasier</I></A>, and <A HREF
="http://www.fox.com/kingofthehill/index
.html"><I>King of the Hill</I></A>.</P>

<P>
<B><FONT COLOR="#87CEFA">Favorite Movies:</FONT>
</B> <A HREF="http://www.meninblack.com/main.html">
<I>Men In Black</I></A>, <A HREF="http://www
.missionimpossible.com/"><I>Mission Impossible</I></A>,
and <A HREF="http://www.starwars.com/episode-v/">
<I>The Empire Strikes Back</I></A>.</P>

<P>
<B><FONT COLOR="#87CEFA">Heroes:</FONT></B>
My heroes are <A HREF="http://www.fgi.net/~db
watty/eric.htm">Eric Clapton</A> (the greatest blues
guitarist ever), <A HREF="http://www.idsoftware.com/
corporate/idhist.html">John Carmack</A> (creator of
<I>Quake</I>), and <A HREF="http://www.bootnet.com/
youaskedforit/lip_linux_manifesto.html">Linus Torvalds
</A> (creator of <I>Linux</I>).

<CENTER>
<IMG SRC="http://www.redwall.org/images/rainbow.gif"
WIDTH="85%" HEIGHT="1" ALT="Rainbow-colored
divider"></CENTER>

<A HREF="MAILTO:dave@redwall.org"><IMG SRC=
"http://www.redwall.org/images/Email.gif" WIDTH="68"
HEIGHT="32" ALIGN="left" BORDER="0" ALT="E-mail
Hyperlink"></A>

©1998 Dave

</P>

</BODY>
</HTML>

Figure 14

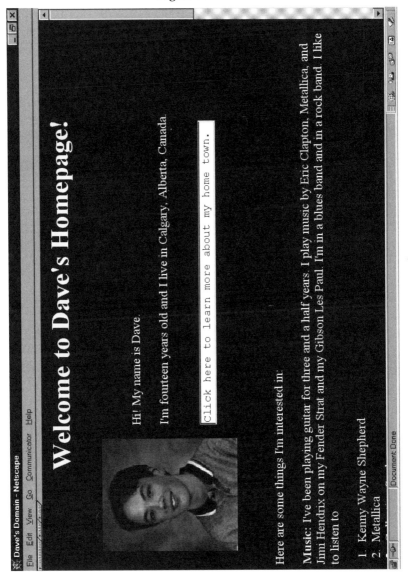

Chapter 8
Animated Images

8.1 Introduction To Animated Images

Twinkling stars can set the stage for a web page on space travel or a web page on nursery rhymes. Hot air balloons floating upward will have equal appeal on a child's web page and on a web page for balloonists. Animated Images can be functional too. They can draw attention to important features of a web page such as e-mail hyperlinks, guestbook hyperlinks, or advertising banners.

An animated image file combines a series of images, each a little different from the one before it, and flips through them to give the appearance of movement. Though animated images can be quite sophisticated, they are easy to use. They are just GIF images which are used in the same way other GIF images are. Be careful not to overdo animation; it can be distracting.

8.2 Downloading Animated Images

The easiest way to obtain animated images is to download them from free animated image libraries on the Internet:

Arg! Cartoon Animation
http://www.artie.com/

Animation Factory
http://www.animfactory.com/

Animated GIF Gallery
http://www.rogersgifs.com/graphics.html

Clipart Castle's Animated Gif Fantasy
http://www.clipartcastle.com/animatedgifs.htm

ScreamDesign - Free Animated GIF Images
http://www.screamdesign.com/graphics/webgraphics/
free/agifs/index.html

Animated GIFs Library
http://animatedgif.net/index.html

Search Topics: Free Animated Images
                 Free Animated GIFs

It's also possible to download an animated image directly from a web page in the same way you download a regular image directly from a web page. The process and 'netiquette described in Chapter 5.8 are the same.

8.3 Creating Animated Images

You don't have to be artistic to be creative. If drawing isn't one of your talents, you can work with text, a clip art image, or a scanned image to create your own animated image. First choose and load an image. Then modify the image to create a series of images which show the object in a slightly different position each time. "Cut and Paste" works well for this. Be careful not to change the position of the image too much from one image to the next or the motion of your finished animated image will be choppy.

Once you have a series of images you're happy with it's time to combine them into a single GIF image file. Download GIF Construction Set as explained in Appendix A and install it. Don't worry about getting your image perfect the first time. It's very easy to go back and edit an image once it's created.

1. Open GIF Construction Set.
2. Hold down the Control key and press the "A" key. This will open the Animation Wizard window. Click Next.
3. Choose "Yes, for use with a web page" and click Next.

4. Choose "Loop indefinitely" and click Next.
5. Choose "Matched to super pallette" and click Next.
6. Set the time delay between frames at 100 hundredths of a second and click Next.
7. Click Select. Then choose the directory your image files are in. Select the image files you wish to use. (You can select several files at once by holding down the Control key while clicking on the image files to highlight them.) Click Open to open those files in GIF Construction Set. Click Cancel in the Open window once you have opened all the files you wish to use. (If you miss a file you need, just click Select again and add the files you need. Similarly if you added a file you don't need, click on it to highlight it and click Delete.) Click Next.
8. Click Done. The Animation Wizard window will close and a list will be shown in the main GIF Construction Set window. The list will include a header, a loop block, a control block for each image, and the images you selected. (The control block sets the time delay between one image and the next, and allows the image background to be made transparent. The loop block sets the number of loops through which the animation will run.) You can edit any of these lines by double-clicking on them to open an Edit window. Try double-clicking on the loop block. When the Edit window opens change the number of "iterations" (loops) to "3". Click OK then click View to test your animated image. When done, right click anywhere on the screen to return to the list.
9. Click on File in the upper left corner of the window, then click on Save As in the drop-down menu, and choose a directory and File Name. Click OK. Then click Exit.
10. To edit an animated image, open it in GIF Construction Set.

Dave's Advice: To make an animated image background transparent you must edit **each** control block and set the transparent color to the background color. To do this, double-click the control block line to open its Edit window. Click beside "Transparent color". Click on the Dropper button. Put the Dropper over the background and click. Set the "Remove by" box to "Background". Click Okay, and you're finished.

Chapter 9
Sound

9.1 Introduction To Web Page Sound

Adding sound to your web page can add a totally new dimension to your visitors' experience. You might want to personalize your web page with a simple audio welcome message. You might want to add sound effects like birds chirping in the forest, a stream flowing through the mountains, or waves breaking on the seashore. Or you might want to play background music to set the mood. If you're a musician you might even want to add a jukebox to your web page so visitors can sample your talent.

Sound files are available from free sound file libraries on the Internet. They can also be created easily by plugging a microphone, tape recorder, or your home stereo into the "Line In" jack or the "Mic" jack on your sound card on the back of your computer. Save the sound as a WAV file using Windows Sound Recorder or as an AIFF file using Apple's Sound Manager. AIFF files can be converted to WAV files using SoundAPP, a freeware program which can be downloaded at

---

http://www-cs-students.stanford.edu/~franke/SoundApp/ or ConvertMachine, a ten dollar shareware program available at http://www.kagi.com/rod/

9.2 Adding Sound To Web Pages

You can add sound to your web page using the hyperlink: **<A HREF="sound.wav"**>name of the sound file**</A>** If the visitor's Internet browser has the necessary audio plug-in installed, clicking the hyperlink will load and play the sound file. Netscape, for example, comes with a plug-in which can play WAV, AIFF, and MIDI files. (MIDI is a digital sound file format which is popular for background music. It uses synthesized musical instruments and has very small files which load quickly.)

> **Dave's Advice:** It's a good idea to indicate the size and format of your sound file on your web page so visitors can determine if their browser has the required plug-in and estimate how long it will take for their browser to load the file. (The average dial-up Internet connection downloads files at 3 Kb/second.)

A better way to add sound to your web page is to use the **<EMBED>** tag which works the same way for sound that the **<IMG>** tag does for images. **<EMBED>** will load a sound player onto your web page when you insert the HTML code **<EMBED SRC="sound.wav" HEIGHT="60" WIDTH="144" AUTOSTART="False" LOOP="0" HIDDEN="False"> </EMBED>** The **HEIGHT** and **WIDTH** attributes set the size of the sound player image on your web page. If **AUTOSTART** is set to "True", sound will play as soon as the sound file is loaded. If **AUTOSTART** is set to "False", sound will play only after the visitor clicks the Play button. **LOOP** sets the number of times the sound file will be played. If **HIDDEN** is set to "False" the sound player will be visible on the web page. If it's set to "True" the sound player will be hidden, as you'd want it to be to when playing background sound on your web page. You can also add the attributes **ALIGN, HSPACE,** and **VSPACE** to specify the position of the sound player image on your web page.

Some versions of Internet Explorer cannot interpret the **<EMBED>** tag, so it's best to add the following code on the next line after the **</EMBED>** closing tag so that viewers using

---

Internet Explorer will be able to hear the sound too.
<NOEMBED>
<BGSOUND SRC="sound.wav" LOOP="1">
</NOEMBED>

9.3 Downloading Sound Files

Sound files can be downloaded from free sound file libraries on the Internet. Here are the URLs of some popular online WAV file libraries:

SOUND America
http://soundamerica.com/

Earth Station 1
http://www.earthstation1.com/

The Daily.WAV
http://www.dailywav.com/

ScreamDesign - Free Sound Files
http://www.screamdesign.com/multimedia/sound/free/index.html

http://www.angelfire.com/mo/keytrax/index.html

Search Topics: Free WAV Files
                 WAV Libraries

and here are the URLs of some popular online MIDI file libraries:

Laura's MIDI Heaven
http://www.laurasmidiheaven.com/

MIDI World
http://midiworld.com/index.htm

Ifni MIDI Music
http://www.ifni.com/midi/

Brian's High Quality MIDI Collection
http://www.uidaho.edu/~imho9431/midi/midi.html

John Roache's Ragtime MIDI Library
http://members.aol.com/ragtimers/index.html

Search Topics: Free MIDI Files
                 MIDI LIbraries

Dave's Advice: If you wish to add copyrighted music to your web page you must obtain the written permission of both the composer and the performer.

Chapter 10
Tables

10.1 Introduction To Web Page Tables

With HTML, neither the tab key nor the space bar will align text or images. This factor makes it difficult to arrange even the simplest web page layout such as adding page margins. Fortunately this problem can be overcome by using tables.

A table is a chart in which information is grouped into columns and rows. In the real world, tables are usually filled with data (numbers). On the Internet, tables can be used in the conventional way to present data but are more often used to create a Table Of Contents. Tables can also be used for web page layout, to place blank space on a web page.

10.2 Tables Of Contents

To create a Table of Contents start with the HTML tags **<TABLE>** and **</TABLE>**. The tags **<TR>** and **</TR>** are placed between the **<TABLE>** tags to create each table row. The tags **<TD>** and **</TD>** (table data) are then inserted between the table row tags to make each table cell into which the data is placed. Here is the code for a simple Table of Contents:

```
<TABLE>
<TR>
<TD> Chapter One</TD>
<TD> Chapter Two</TD>
<TD> Chapter Three</TD></TR>
<TR>
<TD> Chapter Four</TD>
<TD> Chapter Five</TD>
<TD> Chapter Six</TD></TR>
</TABLE>
```

which gives a three column by two row table like this:

| Chapter One | Chapter Two | Chapter Three |
| Chapter Four | Chapter Five | Chapter Six |

Tables can be aligned left, center, or right on a web page by adding the **ALIGN** attribute to the **<TABLE>** opening tag:

```
<TABLE ALIGN="left">
```

A caption (a title) can be added to the table with the tags **<CAPTION>** and **</CAPTION>** placed on the next line after the **<TABLE>** opening tag. The **ALIGN** attribute can be used to place the caption at either the top or the bottom of the table:

```
<CAPTION ALIGN="top">Table of Contents</CAPTION>
```

Here's the source code for our Table of Contents with caption, alignment, and hyperlinks added:

```
<TABLE ALIGN="center">
<CAPTION ALIGN="top">Table of Contents</CAPTION>
<TR>
<TD><A HREF="http://www.redwall.org/chapter1.html">
Chapter One</A></TD>
<TD><A HREF="http://www.redwall.org/chapter2.html">
Chapter Two</A></TD>
<TD><A HREF="http://www.redwall.org/chapter3.html">
Chapter Three</A></TD></TR>
<TR>
<TD><A HREF="http://www.redwall.org/chapter4.html">
Chapter Four</A></TD>
<TD><A HREF="http://www.redwall.org/chapter5.html">
Chapter Five</A></TD>
<TD><A HREF="http://www.redwall.org/chapter6.html">
Chapter Six</A></TD></TR>
</TABLE>
```

which gives a Table of Contents with built-in hyperlinks:

Table of Contents

Chapter 3.7 describes how to upgrade these hyperlinks to image hyperlinks. Chapter 6.3 explains how to add background images to tables, while Chapter 4.5 shows how to add color.

10.3 Data Tables

To post a tour schedule for your favorite rock band or to give statistics for your baseball team, use a data table to present the information. Visit http://www.redwall.org/dave/tour.html to see how I use a data table to post Brian Jacques' Tour Schedule.

To complement the basic HTML table tags covered in Chapter 10.2, several attributes are available to enhance the appearance of tables. Information within individual cells can be aligned left, center, or right by adding the **ALIGN** attribute to the **<TD>** opening tag:

<TD ALIGN="left">

Data can also be aligned top, middle, or bottom by adding the **VALIGN** attribute to the **<TD>** opening tag:

<TD ALIGN="left" VALIGN="top">

The **HEIGHT** attribute can be added to the **<TR>** opening tag to fine tune the height of a row (measured in pixels):

<TR HEIGHT="10">

The attributes **COLSPAN** and **ROWSPAN** enable table cells to span more than one column and/or more than one row. Here's how to specify how many columns and how many rows a table cell is to span:

<TD COLSPAN="3" ROWSPAN="2">

> **Dave's Advice: COLSPAN** and **ROWSPAN** are especially helpful when using different size images as image hyperlinks in a Table of Contents.

Added to the **<TABLE>** opening tag, the attributes **HSPACE** and **VSPACE** set the amount of horizonal space and vertical space between a table and the text flowing around it, measured in pixels:

<TABLE HSPACE="15" VSPACE="20">

BORDER can be used to place a border around a table:

<TABLE BORDER="5">

where 5 specifies the border thickness measured in pixels.

CELLPADDING sets the amount of padding (blank space) within each cell between the cell contents and the cell border, measured in pixels. CELLSPACING sets the width of the border between cells, measured in pixels.

> **Dave's Advice:** When setting up a table, color the cells and border of the table temporarily while deciding on the right settings for **BORDER**, **CELLPADDING** and **CELL-SPACING**. This will make the interaction of these three attributes easier to understand. Chapter 4.5 explains how to color table borders and table cells.

10.4 Web Page Margins

To set equal margins on the top, bottom, and sides of a web page, place the body of the web page within a one-celled table, and use the **CELLSPACING** attribute to set the margin width, measured in pixels, this way:

```
<HTML>
<HEAD>
<TITLE>The title of your page</TITLE>
</HEAD>
<BODY>

<TABLE WIDTH="100%" CELLSPACING="25">
<TR>
<TD>
The body of your page
</TD>
</TR>
</TABLE>

</BODY>
</HTML>
```

Figure 15 shows a screen print of our web page with margins added to it using this HTML code.

10.5 Web Page Layout

The most important design element on a web page is blank space. Careful placing of blank space can make a web page more attractive and easier to read. Variety in the placement of blank space can make a web page more interesting. Magazines use a multi-column layout which also works well for web pages. A page can have two, three, or even four columns. The columns can be different widths. The columns can contain

Figure 15

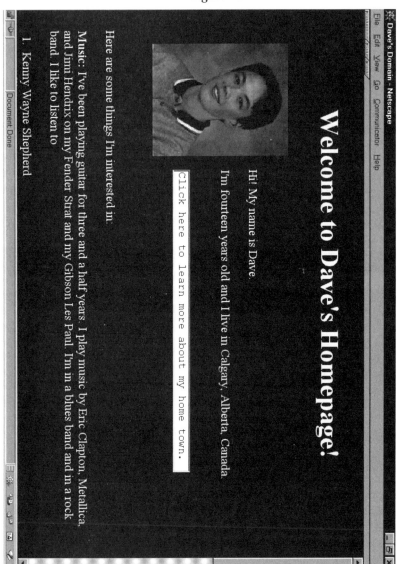

titles, text, images, or blank space. The setup doesn't remain static. It changes as the topics change. Here's how it's done:

1. Set the width of the table in pixels with the **WIDTH** attribute: **<TABLE WIDTH="600">**
   or as a percentage of the size of the screen:
   <TABLE WIDTH="75%">
2. Set the **BORDER** attribute equal to zero, to override any browser default settings.
   <TABLE WIDTH="600" BORDER="0">
3. Add the **WIDTH** attribute to each **<TD>** opening tag to set the width of each column as a percentage of the width of the table: **<TD WIDTH="40%">**
   This setting is done just once for each column, usually in the first row.
4. Together, it looks like this:
   <TABLE WIDTH="600" BORDER="0">
   <TR>
   <TD WIDTH="40%"><!-- this cell is blank --></TD>
   <TD WIDTH="60%">page content **</TD>**
   </TR>
   </TABLE>

> **Dave's Advice:** I used an HTML comment in the last example. An HTML comment looks like this:
> **<!-- comment -->**
> where "comment" is replaced by the comment you wish to make, such as "this cell is blank". An HTML comment helps you to follow HTML source code when you're checking it, but it doesn't show up in a browser. It can be used anywhere in an HTML document.

> **Dave's Advice:** You can vertically align the top line of text in all columns of the same row by adding the attribute **VALIGN** to the **<TR>** opening tag, and setting it eaual to "baseline" like this:
> **<TR VALIGN="baseline">**
> This technique is useful when two columns contain text, with paragraph titles placed in the left column and paragraph content in the right column.

Here's an example of how to code a web page using both two-column and three-column setups with changing placement of content among the columns:

```
<HTML>
<HEAD>
<TITLE>The title of your page</TITLE>
</HEAD>
<BODY>

<!-- begin: text in center column of three columns -->
<TABLE WIDTH="600" BORDER="0">
<TR>
<TD WIDTH="20%"><!-- this cell is blank --></TD>
<TD WIDTH="60%">The first section of text</TD>
<TD WIDTH="20%"><!-- this cell is blank --></TD>
</TR>
</TABLE>
<!-- end: text in center column of three columns -->

<!-- begin: image in left column with text in right column -->
<TABLE WIDTH="600" BORDER="0">
<TR VALIGN="top">
<TD WIDTH="50%" ALIGN="center">
<IMG SRC="http://www.redwall.org/dave.jpg"></TD>
<TD WIDTH="50%">The second section of text</TD>
</TR>
</TABLE>
<!-- end: image in left column with text in right column -->

<!-- begin: text in right column of two columns -->
<TABLE WIDTH="600" BORDER="0">
<TR>
<TD WIDTH="50%"><!-- this cell is blank --></TD>
<TD WIDTH="50%">The third section of text</TD>
</TR>
</TABLE>
<!-- end: text in right column of two columns -->

</BODY>
</HTML>
```

Figure 16 shows the source code for our web page with a multi-column layout. **Figure 17** shows how this layout looks when viewed in Netscape. It's on the web at:
http://www.erinbooks.com/resource/Figure17.html

Figure 16

```
<HTML>
<HEAD>
<TITLE>Dave's Domain</TITLE>
<SCRIPT LANGUAGE="JavaScript">
<!--

var delayCC=150;
var messageCC="My home town is Canada's fifth largest
city with a population of 800,000.    It's located on the Bow
River where the prairies meet the foothills of the Rocky
Mountains.    It's the gateway to Banff National Park.
Calgary is the oil and gas capital of Canada.       It's
surrounded by grain farms and cattle ranches.     The
Winter Olympic Games were held here in 1988.      The
World Police and Fire Games were held here in 1997.";
var timerCC=0;
var alignRightCC=0;
while (alignRightCC++<45) messageCC=" "+messageCC;
function BannerCC( )
{document.bannerCC.bannerField.value=messageCC.substring
(timerCC++,messageCC.length);
if (timerCC==messageCC.length) timerCC=0;
setTimeout ("BannerCC( )",delayCC);}
//-->
</SCRIPT>
<STYLE>A {text-decoration: none}</STYLE>
</HEAD>

<BODY BGCOLOR="#000000" TEXT="#D2B48C" LINK=
"#7FFFD4" VLINK="#20B2AA" BACKGROUND="http://
www.redwall.org/images/blkmagic.gif">


<!-- BEGIN TABLE -->
<TABLE WIDTH="100%" BORDER="0">
<TR>
<TD WIDTH="5%"><!-- this cell is blank --></TD>
<TD WIDTH="24%"></TD>
<TD WIDTH="56%"></TD>
<TD WIDTH="15%"><!-- this cell is blank --></TD>
</TR>


<TR>
<TD><!-- column 1 --></TD>
<TD COLSPAN="2"><!-- columns 2 and 3 -->
```

Figure 16 (continued)

```
<CENTER><H1><FONT COLOR="#87CEFA">Welcome to
Dave's Homepage!</FONT></H1></CENTER>

<IMG SRC="http://www.redwall.org/images/Dave.jpg"
WIDTH="137" HEIGHT="170" ALIGN="left" HSPACE=
"25" VSPACE="25" ALT="Photograph of Dave">
<BR>
<BR>
<BR>

<P>
Hi! My name is Dave.</P>

<P>
I'm fourteen years old and I live in <A HREF="http://www.
visitor.calgary.ab.ca/">Calgary</A>, Alberta, Canada.</P>
<BR>

<FORM NAME="bannerCC">
<INPUT TYPE="text" NAME="bannerField" SIZE=45
VALUE="Click here to learn more about my home town."
onFocus="{BannerCC( )}">
</FORM>
<BR>
<BR>
<BR>

<P>
Here are some things I'm interested in:</P>
</TD>
<TD><!-- column 4 --></TD>
</TR>


<TR VALIGN="baseline">
<TD><!-- column 1 --></TD>
<TD ALIGN="right"><!-- column 2 --><BR>
<B><FONT COLOR="#87CEFA">Music:</FONT></B>
</TD>
<TD><!-- column 3 --><BR>
I've been playing guitar for three and a half years. I play
music by <A HREF="http://www.fgi.net/~dbwatty
/eric.htm">Eric Clapton</A>, <A HREF="http://www.
metallica.com">Metallica</A>, and <A HREF="http://
www.jimi-hendrix.com">Jimi Hendrix</A> on my <A
HREF="http://www.fender.com/electricguitars/strats/
americanseries/amerstrat.html">Fender Strat</A> and my
```

Figure 16 (continued)

```
<A HREF="http://www.gibson.com/products/epiphone/
inst/Les-Paul/ENST.html">Gibson Les Paul</A>. I'm in a
blues band and in a rock band. I like to listen to
<OL>
<LI><A     HREF="http://www.kwsband.com">Kenny
Wayne Shepherd</A></LI>
<LI><A HREF="http://www.metallica.com">Metallica
</A></LI>
<LI><A HREF="http://www.csoul.com">Collective Soul
</A></LI>
<LI><A HREF="http://www.rammstein.de">Rammstein
</A></LI>
</OL></TD>
<TD><!-- column 4 --></TD>
</TR>


<TR VALIGN="baseline">
<TD><!-- column 1 --></TD>
<TD ALIGN="right"><!-- column 2 --><BR>
<B><FONT COLOR="#87CEFA">Books:</FONT></B>
</TD>
<TD><!-- column 3 --><BR>
<A HREF="http://www.redwall.org/dave/jacques.html">
Brian Jacques</A> is my favorite author. I also enjoy books
by <A HREF="http://www.hipiers.com">Piers Anthony
</A> and <A HREF="http://www.friend.ly.net/scoop/
biographies/alexanderlloyd/index.html">Lloyd
Alexander</A>.</TD>
<TD><!-- column 4 --></TD>
</TR>


<TR VALIGN="baseline">
<TD><!-- column 1 --></TD>
<TD ALIGN="right"><!-- column 2 --><BR>
<B><FONT COLOR="#87CEFA">Sports:</FONT></B>
</TD>
<TD><!-- column 3 --><BR>
I like biking in the summer, and snowboarding in the winter.
I played Little League Baseball and I've tried
<UL>
<LI>basketball</LI>
<LI>soccer</LI>
```

Figure 16 (continued)

```
<LI>fencing</LI>
<LI>water-skiing</LI>
</UL></TD>
<TD><!-- column 4 --></TD>
</TR>

<TR VALIGN="baseline">
<TD><!-- column 1 --></TD>
<TD ALIGN="right"><!-- column 2 --><BR>
<B><FONT COLOR="#87CEFA">Hobbies:</FONT></B>
</TD>
<TD><!-- column 3 --><BR>
```
I like playing games on the Internet, computer programming, <A HREF="http://www.foosball.com/"> foosball</A>, and <A HREF="http://www.capture theflag.com/">paintball</A>.</TD>
```
<TD><!-- column 4 --></TD>
</TR>

<TR VALIGN="baseline">
<TD><!-- column 1 --></TD>
<TD ALIGN="right"><!-- column 2 --><BR>
<B><FONT COLOR="#87CEFA">School:</FONT></B>
</TD>
<TD><!-- column 3 --><BR>
```
I'm in the ninth grade in junior high school. I play guitar in the stage band.</TD>
```
<TD><!-- column 4 --></TD>
</TR>

<TR VALIGN="baseline">
<TD><!-- column 1 --></TD>
<TD ALIGN="right"><!-- column 2 --><BR>
<B><FONT COLOR="#87CEFA">Favorite  Comics:
</FONT></B></TD>
<TD><!-- column 3 --><BR>
<A HREF="http://www.foxtrot.com"><I>Foxtrot</I></A>
and <A HREF="http://www.calvinandhobbes.com"><I>
```
Calvin and Hobbes</I></A>.</TD>
```
<TD><!-- column 4 --></TD>
</TR>
```

Figure 16 (continued)

```
<TR VALIGN="baseline">
<TD><!-- column 1 --></TD>
<TD ALIGN="right"><!-- column 2 --><BR>
 <B><FONT COLOR="#87CEFA">Favorite TV:</FONT>
</B></TD>
<TD><!-- column 3 --><BR>
<A HREF="http://www.theX-Files.com/"><I>X-Files</I>
</A>, <A HREF="http://www.paramount.com/television/
frasier/"><I>Frasier</I></A>, and <A HREF="http://
www.fox.com/kingofthehill/index.html"><I>King of the
Hill</I></A>.</TD>
<TD><!-- column 4 --></TD>
</TR>


<TR VALIGN="baseline">
<TD><!-- column 1 --></TD>
<TD ALIGN="right"><!-- column 2 --><BR>
<B><FONT COLOR="#87CEFA">Favorite Movies:</FONT>
</B></TD>
<TD><!-- column 3 --><BR>
<A HREF="http://www.meninblack.com/main.html"><I>
Men In Black</I></A>, <A HREF="http://www.mission
impossible.com"><I>Mission Impossible</I></A>, and
<A HREF="http://www.starwars.com/episode-v/"><I>The
Empire Strikes Back</I></A>.</TD>
<TD><!-- column 4 --></TD>
</TR>


<TR VALIGN="baseline">
<TD><!-- column 1 --></TD>
<TD ALIGN="right"><!-- column 2 --><BR>
<B><FONT COLOR="#87CEFA">Heroes:</FONT></B>
</TD>
<TD><!-- column 3 --><BR>
My heroes are <A HREF="http://www.fgi.net/~dbwatty/
eric.htm">Eric Clapton</A> (the greatest blues guitarist
ever), <A HREF="http://www.idsoftware.com/corporate/
idhist.html">John Carmack</A> (creator of <I>Quake
</I>), and <A HREF="http://www.bootnet.com/you
askedforit/lip_linux_manifesto.html">Linus Torvalds
</A> (creator of <I>Linux</I>).</TD>
<TD><!-- column 4 --></TD>
</TR>
```

Figure 16 (continued)

```
<TR>
<TD><!-- column 1 --></TD>
<TD><!-- column 2 --></TD>
<TD><!-- column 3 -->
<BR>
<CENTER>
<IMG SRC="http://www.redwall.org/images/rainbow.gif"
WIDTH="85%" HEIGHT="1" ALT="Rainbow-colored
divider"></CENTER></TD>
<TD><!-- column 4 --></TD>
</TR>

<TR>
<TD><!-- column 1 --></TD>
<TD><!-- column 2 -->
<BR>
<A HREF="MAILTO:dave@redwall.org"><IMG SRC=
"http://www.redwall.org/images/Email.gif" WIDTH="68"
HEIGHT="32" ALIGN="left" BORDER="0" ALT="E-mail
Hyperlink"></A>
<BR>
<BR>
&copy;1998 Dave
<BR>
</TD>
<TD><!-- column 3 --></TD>
<TD><!-- column 4 --></TD>
</TR>

</TABLE>
<!-- END TABLE -->

</BODY>
</HTML>
```

Figure 17

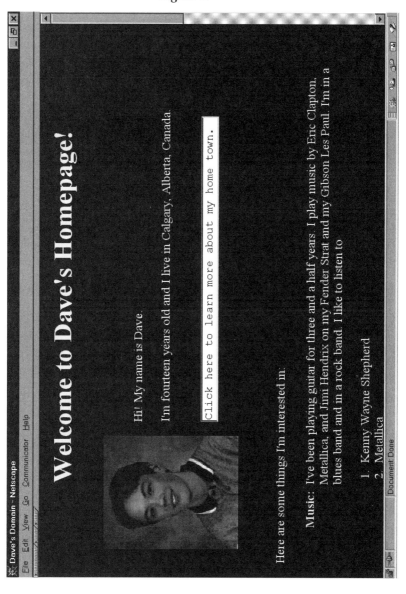

Chapter 11
Multi-page Web Sites

11.1 Introduction to Multi-page Web Sites

As you add more features to your web page, it will take longer for browsers to load. Once the load time is more than about twenty seconds using a 28.8 modem, visitors will become impatient and may move on to someone else's web page rather than waiting for yours to load. It's time to convert your web page to a multi-page web site. Start with a simple homepage as the "front door". The homepage must capture visitors' interest quickly. It will introduce your web site and will provide links to your other web pages, each covering a related topic and each small enough to download within twenty seconds. Your web pages should be tied together with a consistent appearance and with a good system for navigating between them.

11.2 Consistent Appearance

It's important that web pages on a multi-page web site have a consistent appearance so that visitors can easily recognize when they're on the web site and when hyperlinks have taken them off the web site. Visitors will become more familiar with the system for navigating between web pages if it looks and works the same way on every web page.

One way to achieve consistency is to use the same header and footer on every web page. A header is the top portion of a web page which contains the name of the web site, a logo, and perhaps a Table of Contents. A footer is the lower portion of the web page which contains copyright information and an e-mail address. Design your homepage and save a copy of it as a file named template.htm. Each time you wish to create a new page, load template.htm and save it under the new file name. Then replace the information on the web page with the relevant information for the new topic, and save the file again. A template is especially useful when tables are used and HTML code becomes complicated.

If your Internet Service Provider is using Apache software to run its web server, there's an easier way to use headers and footers on your web site. Apache allows files to be inserted in the BODY section of an HTML document using a command called **#include file**. Updating a Table of Contents is much easier when it's part of a header or footer which can be inserted in all your web pages, because only one file has to be updated when there's a change. The quickest way to find out if the **#include file** will work on your web site is to try it.

Create a header file by typing the information you want to display in the header, and save the file as "header.htm". Include only the header information itself. Don't include the tags **<HTML>**, **<HEAD>**, **<TITLE>**, **<BODY>** or their closing tags. The original header file for the Redwall Abbey web site looked like this:
<CENTER>
**<IMG SRC="ABBEY.gif" WIDTH="450" HEIGHT="163" ALT="Redwall logo">
**
</CENTER>

Store the header file on the web server in the same directory as your web page files. Then insert the following code into each web page as the first line after the **<BODY>** opening tag
<!--#include file="header.htm"-->

A footer file is set up the same way as a header file, with **<!--#include file="footer.htm"-->** inserted at the bottom of each web page as the last line before the **</BODY>** closing tag. If visitors check your source code in a browser, the contents of the header and the footer files will have already been inserted into your web page. There is no indication that the **#include file** command was used.

> **Dave's Advice:** If you're able to use the **#include file** command on your web site, it can be used to insert any file anywhere between the **<BODY>** and **</BODY>** tags of a web page. Just substitute the name of the file for **"footer.htm"** in the **#include file** command. I use an **#include file** for the book list on the pages which make up The Redwall Library at http://www.redwall.org/dave/library.html because it must be updated frequently.

In my next book I'll be covering the use of Style Sheets, a more sopisticated way to ensure that web pages on a multi-page web site maintain a consistent appearance.

11.3 Navigation

Once you've converted your web page to a multi-page web site, you'll need to provide an easy way for visitors to navigate around your web site. You can use a Table of Contents which I covered in Chapters 3.4 and 10.2, or you can use a Site Map which is just a separate web page giving a detailed Table of Contents with hyperlinks built in.

If you want to set up a Site Map, I suggest you use a table and start with a list of all your web pages. Organize them by topic, and use the Heading tags **<H3>** and **</H3>** for each topic. Then convert the list to hyperlinks. Add a hyperlink to your Site Map from each of your web pages, and you're finished.

If we expanded our sample web page into a multi-page web site, a Site Map for it would look something like this:

<u>Homepage</u>
<u>Music</u> <u>Books</u> <u>Sports</u> <u>Hobbies</u> <u>School</u> <u>Interests</u> <u>Heroes</u>

Chapter 12
Image Maps

12.1 Introduction To Image Maps

An Image Map is either a Table of Contents or a Site Map presented as an image, with several hyperlink hot spots built into it. Clicking the hot spots links the viewer to different destination URLs the same way clicking a hyperlink in a standard Table of Contents or Site Map does. Image Maps can add interest and atmosphere to a web site. However, like all graphics, Image Maps are large files which are slow to load.

12.2 Adding Image Maps To Web Pages

The first step in creating an Image Map is to choose or design the image you wish to use. Then determine what the co-ordinates are for each section of the image which is to be used as a hot spot. You can learn what these co-ordinates are by loading the image into Paint Shop Pro and moving your mouse over the image. The co-ordinates of your mouse cursor are shown on the left side of the task bar at the bottom of the window just above the Windows Start button.

Place the image where you'd liket it on your web page using the **IMG** tag and the **SRC** attribute:
<IMG SRC="image.gif">

Add the **USEMAP** attribute to the **IMG** tag to indicate which Image Map will be used to place the hot spots on this image:
<IMG SRC="image.gif" USEMAP ="#map_name">

Set **BORDER** equal to "0" to eliminate the usual colored hyperlink border around the image:
<IMG SRC="image.gif" USEMAP="#map_name"BORDER ="0">

Now, define the Image Map itself using the tags **<MAP>** and **</MAP>**. The first step is to add the **NAME** attribute to the **<MAP>** tag to indicate which Image Map is being defined:
<MAP NAME="map_name">
</MAP>

The second step is to define each Image Map hot spot using the **AREA** tag and the **SHAPE** attribute to specify the hot spot shape as either a rectangle, a point, a circle, or a polygon. Rectangle is the default shape when no shape is specified.
<MAP NAME="map_name">
<AREA SHAPE="RECT">
<AREA SHAPE="POINT">
<AREA SHAPE="CIRCLE">
<AREA SHAPE="POLY">
</MAP>

When hot spots overlap, the hot spot listed first will take precedence over the hot spot listed second, and the hot spot listed second will take precedence over the hot spot listed third, and so on.

The third step is to specify the hot spot co-ordinates using the **COORDS** attribute based on the shape specified with the **SHAPE** attribute:

- **RECT** - give the co-ordinates of the upper left corner and the lower right corner.
- **POINT** - give the co-ordinates of the point.
- **CIRCLE** - give the co-ordinates of the center point of the circle, and give the radius of the circle in pixels.
- **POLY** - give the co-ordinates of a starting point, and of each major point around the outline of the polygon. (Draw a point-to-point outline around the polygon.)

To make the remainder of the image the default hot spot, set **SHAPE** equal to **DEFAULT** and omit the **COORDS** attribute:
`<AREA SHAPE="DEFAULT">`

The fourth step is to add a hyperlink to each hot spot using the **HREF** attribute to specify the destination URL:
`<AREA SHAPE="RECT" COORDS="0,0, 20,35"`
`HREF="http://www.redwall.org/page1.html">`

The fifth step is to add an **ALT** attribute to each hot spot, to identify it for those whose browsers aren't recognizing images.

Here is the HTML code for an Image Map named "tango" which uses an image named "tangerine.gif": It would be inserted into an HTML file wherever the Image Map "tango" is to be placed.

```
<IMG SRC="http://www.redwall.org/dave/tangerine.gif"
USEMAP ="#tango" BORDER="0">
<MAP NAME="tango">
<AREA SHAPE="POINT" COORDS="378,54"
HREF="http://www.redwall.org/page1.html"
ALT="Page One">
<AREA SHAPE="RECT" COORDS="0,0, 20,35"
HREF="http://www.redwall.org/page2.html"
ALT="Page Two">
<AREA SHAPE="CIRCLE" COORDS="45,70, 12"
HREF="http://www.redwall.org/page3.html"
ALT="Page Three">
<AREA SHAPE="POLY" COORDS="45,60, 70,32, 85,43,
107,93, 96,110, 67,134, 53,77"
HREF="http://www.redwall.org/page4.html"
ALT="Page Four">
<AREA SHAPE="DEFAULT"
HREF="http://www.redwall.org/page5.html"
ALT="Page One">
</MAP>
```

> **Dave's Advice:** One alternative to Image Maps uses a table to place several images adjacent to each other, with each image set up as an image hyperlink. **BORDER**, **CELLPADDING**, and **CELLSPACING** are all set equal to "0" so that the images butt against each other. **COLSPAN** and **ROWSPAN** are used to adjust the table for images of different shapes and sizes. Then each image is set up as an image hyperlink with its own **ALT**.

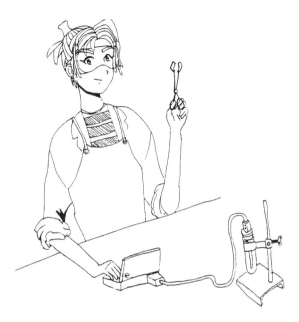

Chapter 13
Web Gadgets

13.1 Introduction To Web Gadgets

Web gadgets are web-based services which add special features to your web page to make it more interesting and more interactive. The most popular web gadgets are visitor counters, guest books, form processors, message boards, chat rooms, password-protected areas, web page statistics generators, and URL redirectors.

Usually your Internet Service Provider (ISP) will provide web gadgets written as Common Gateway Interface (CGI) programs. However many ISPs don't offer web gadgets because of the amount of time it takes to set up and maintain them. Fortunately there are several web sites on the Internet which provide and maintain free web gadgets. One of the disadvantages of having a web gadget located on a server other than where your web page is stored is load time of the gadget. Compare competing web sites with this in mind.

Some of the folks who provide web gadgets do so out of the goodness of their hearts. Most do it for profit, usually by selling advertising space on their gadgets. A few are rumored to do it to "lift" the e-mail addresses of visitors to your web page and sell them to advertisers who flood e-mail servers with spam (unwanted junk e-mail). Be careful who you choose.

13.2 Visitor Counters

Visitor Counters keep track of the number of visits your web page receives. They don't actually count the number of visitors; they count the number of visits.

You can choose from many different graphic styles to suit the atmosphere of your web page. Some are just numbers; some are graphics made to look like car odometers; and some are too elaborate for description. Here's where to find them:

Being Seen's Hit Counters
http://www.beseen.com/beseen/free/counters.html

Better Counters
http://www.better-counter.com/

Escati Free Counter
http://www.escati.com/

Free Webpage Hit Counter
http://www.prtracker.com/FreeCounter3.html

The Ultimate Counter
http://counters.qpt.com/

Search Topic: Free Counter

13.3 Guest Books

Guest Books allow visitors to your web page to post a message for everyone to read. Guests are usually prompted to leave their name, hometown, and comments about your web site. You'll be surprised to learn how far away some of your visitors live. Date and time are recorded automatically. I used a Guest Book to ask visitors to The Official Brian Jacques Web Site what their favorite Redwall adventure was and why.

Guest Books can cause frustration because there's always some moron who will post graffiti in your Guest Book. If you have a Guest Book, you should check it every day or two in case there's something that should be erased.

Here are the URLs of websites which provide free Guest Books:

1-2-3 Webtools
http://www.freeguestbooks.com/

Dreambook
http://www.dreambook.com/

Guestpage
http://www.guestpage.com/

htmlGEAR
http://guestworld.tripod.lycos.com/

Phaistos Guestbooks
http://phaistos.forthnet.gr/services/guestbooks/

Search Topic: Free Guest Book

13.4 Form Processors

Placing a Form Processor on your web page allows visitors to provide information which can be e-mailed to you and/or added directly to a database. A Form Processor can be set up to automatically send different replies to the visitor depending on the information he or she provides on the form.

I've used a Form Processor to process club membership applications, to process subscriptions to a newsletter, to run a contest, and to take surveys. These three web sites provide free Form Processors:

Formmail+
http://www.vpdev.com/freestuff/help/formmail.shtml

Freedback
http://Freedback.com/?drweb

Search Topic: Free Form Processor

13.5 Message Boards

A Message Board is the Internet equivalent of a bulletin board. Visitors can post messages on them for others to read. They automatically record and display the time and date the message is posted. They can also be set up to provide an e-mail hyperlink to the person who posted the message.

Here are the URLs of web sites which provide Message Boards:

Beseen's Bulletin Board
http://www.beseen.com/board/index.html

InsideThe Web
http://www.InsideTheWeb.com/create.cgi

Search Topic: Free Message Board

13.6 Chat Rooms

Chat Rooms are web sites where people meet to have a conversation in "real time". Some chat rooms are just Message Boards which are refreshed very frequently. Some chat rooms allow you to see the messages as they're being typed. Some chat rooms actually allow you to talk, if you have a microphone and speakers connected to your computer.

Here's where to find them:

Beseen Chat
http://beseen.com/chat/mr-index.html

Chat@Talk City
http://www.talkcity.com/irc/apply.html

Chat Planet
http://www.chatplanet.com/license.html

ParaChat
http://parachat.com/

Search topic: Free Chat Rooms

13.7 Password-protected Areas

Password-protected areas allow you to restrict access to parts of your web site to people to whom you give a password. The simplest password-protected area uses the same password for everyone, while a better password-protected area uses a different password for each visitor. Elaborate systems can record who used their password and when.

I used several password-protected areas to provide discussion areas for different topics of interest to Redwall Club Members. Here is the URL of a web site which can provide password protection for your web page:

Free Password Protection
http://www.fido7.com/free-cgi/auth/

Search Topic: Free Password Protection

13.8 Statistics Generators

Statistics Generators can provide information about the visitors to your web site. You can learn what country they're from, how they found out about your web site, which part of your web site is the most popular, how many times the same person visits your web site, and much more.

The folks at these web sites offer free web page Statistics Generators:

Counted!
http://www.counted.com/

Cyber Stats
http://www.pagetools.com/cyberstats/admin2.html

Freestats
http://www.freestats.com/

NedStat USA
http://usa.nedstat.net/

Site-Stats
http://www.site-stats.com/

WebTracker
http://www.fxweb.holowww.com/tracker/

Search Topic: Free Web Page Statistics

13.9 URL Redirectors

One difficulty with locating your web page on a free web server is that your page's URL (Internet address) is often both long and difficult to remember. URL Redirectors offer a solution which is the next best thing to having your own Internet domain name, but without the expense. You can combine your creativity with the catchy domain names some Redirectors provide, to come up with an easy to remember URL. Then when visitors visit that URL, they are automatically forwarded to your web page on the free server. Some Redirectors even provide "cloaking" which hides the fact that you are using a redirection service. It appears that you have your own domain name. Visitors are much more likely to return to your web site for a second visit.

Most redirectors can also provide a matching E-mail address.

Here's where to find three of the many free URL Redirectors:

V3 - The Internet Identity Company
http://www.v3.com/v3home.asp

CyberName
http://www.cybername.net/

CJB.NET
http://www.cjb.net/

Search Topic: Free URL Redirection

What's Next?

Now that you're familiar with the technical side of creating a web site, it's time to focus on being creative. It's time to think "outside the box".

In this book I used a basic personal web page to demonstrate some of the tools available for web site creation. It's time to use these tools in unconventional ways. It's time to combine the tips and tricks I've showed you, in unusual ways.

Be original! That's the difference between creating a good web site and creating a great web site.

My next book in this series will explore more advanced techniques including frames, dynamic menus, and cascading style sheets. I'm working on it now.

In the meantime visit my new corner of the web, where I'll provide links to recommended resources plus the Figures used in this book. It's located at:

http://www.erinbooks.com/resource

Appendix A: Software Tools

Netscape Communicator
Netscape Communicator is the web browser I use. It comes with an HTML editor ("Composer") and an FTP program ("Publish") built in. It can be downloaded free from
http://www.netscape.com/download

Internet Explorer
Internet Explorer is included with Windows and is free at
http://www.microsoft.com/windows/ie/download/ie55.htm

TuCows
TuCows is the ultimate source of freeware and shareware related to the Internet, with over 30,000 titles available online. It's not one web site; it's a series of over 400 mirror web sites around the world. TuCows groups shareware, reviews it, and rates it, then provides links to fast download sites. Visit the main site to find out which mirror site is closest to you:
http://www.tucows.com

WS FTP LE
WS FTP LE is the FTP program I recommend, because it's easy to use and it's free. It's also the only freeware FTP program to be awarded TuCows top ("five cow") rating. You can download WS FTP LE from any TuCows site.

Paint Shop Pro
Paint Shop Pro (PSP) can do everything you need to do with images to prepare them for the Internet. It works well with any scanner to acquire images. It can edit and enhance images. PSP can convert images from one format to another, and it comes with Animation Shop which will allow you to animate images. PSP earned TuCows top ("five cow") rating and can be down-loaded for a free trial from TuCows or from
http://www.jasc.com/download_4.asp

GIF Construction Set
I recommend GIF Construction Set because it has an Animation Wizard which makes it very easy to use. At $20 it's less than half the price of it's "five cow" competitors. It can be down-loaded for a free trial from TuCows or from:
http://www.mindworkshop.com/alchemy/gifcon.html

Appendix B: Internet Access

Free Internet access, sponsored by advertising, is now readily available throughout North America and much of Europe. Plans for free services have also been announced for Latin America. Most free Internet Service Providers offer free web space and free e-mail accounts. Here's a list of the current major players.

North America

Address.com
http://www.address.com/main.asp?p=freeinternet&
addressref=mlistwa&clicktrade=

AltaVista FreeAccess
http://www.zdnet.com/downloads/altavista/

FreeLane
http://freelane.excite.com/?AID=900209&PID=348233

FreeWebOntario
http://freewebontario.netfirms.com/

iFreedom
http://www.ifreedom.com/

JUNO
http://dl.www.juno.com/get/web/

LYCOS Free Internet Access
http://free.lycos.com?sourceid=00325861211620350385/

NetZero
http://www.netzero.net/

Europe

AltaVista Deutschland
http://de.altavista.com/freein/

Freewire
http://www.freewire.net/

Tiscali Net
http://www.tiscalinet.be/

Worldwide

Free Internet Access Index
http://www.emailaddresses.com/email_internet.htm

Search Topic: Free Internet Access

Appendix C: Web-based E-mail

Many companies provide free web-based e-mail in return for placing advertising on the page where you retrieve your e-mail. These e-mail services are accessed via an Internet browser rather than by using an e-mail program. You can access your web-based e-mail from any online computer in the world. When you go on vacation or move to a new city, you can still receive your e-mail at the same e-mail address.

Web-based e-mail allows you to create an e-mail address which reveals your personality, but doesn't reveal who you are or where you live.

Here's where to obtain free web-based e-mail.

Netscape WebMail
http://webmail.netscape.com/

Yahoo! Mail
http://mail.yahoo.com/

Yahoo! GeoCities
http://www.geocities.com/join/

HotMail
http://www.hotmail.com/

Juno
http://www.juno.com/whatis_basic.html

Lycos Communications
http://comm.lycos.com/

iName Mail.com
http://www.iname.com/info/intro/index.html

Excite Mail
http://reg.excite.com/mps/login?pname=mail&targeturl=http://mail.excite.com/&brand=xcit

Based in the Philippines, one e-mail service even offers free foreign language e-mail using Chinese, Japanese, Korean, and Thai characters, as well as English:
Kokomosmail.com
http://www.kokomosmail.com/

Search Topic: Free Web-based E-mail

Appendix D: Web Servers

With Banner Ads

Many Internet Service Providers, supported by advertising, offer free web server space. In return for a free place to host your site, you allow your web page to be commercialized with an advertising banner and/or a pop-up advertising window. Before signing up for free web space, find out:

1. How much advertising will be placed on your web page?
2. Will the advertising be offensive to you or your viewers?
3. How much web space will the ISP provide?
4. How quickly will your web pages load?
5. What web gadgets will be provided?

AcmeCity
http://www.acmecity.com/join/index.html

Angelfire
http://angelfire.lycos.com/

Fortune City
http://www.fortunecity.com/

FreeWebSpace
http://www.free-web-space-inc.com/

Homestead
http://www.homestead.com/

Net Citizen
http://NetCitizen.com/

TerraShare
http://www.TerraShare.com/

TopCities.com
http://www.topcities.com/

Tripod
http://www.tripod.lycos.com/

Virtual Avenue
http://www.virtualave.net/index.gsp

Yahoo! GeoCities
http://geocities.yahoo.com/home/

20m Free Web Space
http://www.20m.com/

Search Topic: Free Web Pages

Without Banner Ads

Most visitors to advertising-sponsored web sites quickly tire of pop-up windows and distracting banners. Recognizing this situation, a few Internet Service Providers have come up with new systems which leave your web page untouched. Instead, some of these ISPs e-mail a daily flyer of advertising to you. Others simply provide advertising on their web sites, but not on yours.

AngelCities
http://www.angelcities.com/

Bigstep
http://www.bigstep.com/

Brinkster
http://www.brinkster.com/Join.asp

Cybercities
http://www.cybercities.com/

DotEasy
http://www.doteasy.com/

Freedom2Surf
http://www.f2s.com/free/free%20home.htm

Stas::Net
http://www.stas.net/

Stormloader
http://www.stormloader.com/

The Burgh
http://www.tbns.net/

VeoWeb
http://www.veoweb.com/

Search Topic: Banner Free Web Pages

Appendix E: Uploading Web Pages

Most FTP programs work the same way. Here, I'll show how to set up and use an FTP program called WS FTP LE. It's one of the most popular FTP programs because it works well, it's easy to use, and it's free. Appendix A shows where to obtain it.

Once you've downloaded and installed WS FTP LE, open it. Two dialog boxes will open, one on top of the other. We'll start with the top box, the one titled "Session Properties".

1. The "General" tab should be on top. If it isn't, just click it to bring it to the top.
2. Click the "New" button so you can set up the program to work with a new Internet Service Provider (ISP).
3. Fill in the first blank space, titled "Profile Name" with the name of your ISP ("GeoCities" for example).
4. In the second blank space titled "Host Name/Address" enter your ISP's Internet Protocol (IP) address whether it's a name like "redwall.org" or a numerical address such as "199.175.107.253".
5. The next space titled "Host Type" should already indicate "Automatic Detect". If it doesn't, click on the arrow to the right of the space and select "Automatic Detect".
6. In the next blank space titled "User ID" fill in the user ID your ISP gave you.
7. Similarly, in the next blank space titled "Password" enter the password your ISP gave you.
8. If you use your own computer or a family computer, click the space titled "Save Pwd" and you won't have to type in the password every time you use the FTP program. If you share the computer with others, at school for example, don't save your password or others will be able to change your web page.
9. Click on the "Apply" button to save this information.

Next, click the "Startup" tab.
1. In the first blank space titled "Initial Remote Site Folder" enter the name of the folder (directory) in which your web page will be stored on the web server. This will probably be left blank, but if not, your ISP will tell you what to enter here.
2. In the second blank space titled "Initial Local Folder"

enter the name of the folder (directory) in which your web page is stored on your computer. Most likely this will be something like "C:\WebPages".

3. Click the "Apply" button to save this information.

WS FTP LE is now set up to transfer files between your computer and your ISP's web server. What you see now is what you'll see each time you open WS FTP LE. (Be sure your ISP's name is shown in the box titled "Profile Name". If not, click the arrow to the right of the box and select your ISP's name from the list which will drop down.)

Click the "OK" button of the Session Properties box and it will close. Your computer is now connecting with your ISP's web server. Once the connection is made, you will hear a sound like a train whistle, and the lower panel will show a message ending in the line "226 Transfer Complete". The name of the box will have changed, adding the address of your ISP such as "geocities.com" to "WS_FTP LE" as the box title, to give "WS_FTP LE geocities.com".

You're now ready to upload your web page and any other related files such as image files and sound files to your ISP's web server. The box you're looking at is split into two parts. On the left is the directory where your web page files are stored on your computer. On the right is the directory where your web page files will be stored on your ISP's web server. In between are two arrows, one pointing to the left and one pointing to the right. Down below are three choices: ASCII, Binary, and Auto. Click "Binary" to select it.

To upload a file to the web server click the file in the left column to highlight it. Then click the arrow pointing to the right column. A dialog box titled "Transfer Status" will pop up. It will indicate the name and size of the file being transfered. It will also show the progress of the transfer as the file is being transfered. When the transfer is complete, you'll hear a weird sound effect and the file will be listed in the right column, the one which shows which files are loaded on the ISP's web server.

If by some chance you have uploaded the wrong file, just click the file name in the right column to highlight it, then click the "Delete" button to the right of the right column to delete it. A box titled "Verify Deletion" will appear. Click its "Yes" button.

If you've loaded a file with the three character extender "htm" and you'd like to use the four character extender "html", highlight the file name in the right column and click the "Rename" button to the right of the right column. A dialog box titled "Input" will appear. Enter the new file name and click its "OK" button.

If your home computer should "crash" you can download your web page files from the ISP's web server to your computer by highlighting the files in the right column, and using the arrow button which points to the left.

Once you've uploaded each of your web page files to the web server, click the "Close" button at the bottom left side of the screen. A message will be shown in the lower panel which ends with the line "221 Goodbye". Then click the "Exit" button at the bottom right side of the screen and the FTP program will close.

Appendix F: Search Engines

Once you've uploaded your web page to the 'net, you'll want to let the world know it exists and where to find it. You can accomplish both tasks by registering your web page with Internet search engines. They're databases which index the World Wide Web. Though some of these databases are huge (AltaVista claims to index over 150 million pages), no one database is able to cover more than one-sixth of the Internet.

Web Page Title

Before registering with search engines, review the title of your web page given between the <TITLE> and </TITLE> tags. The title here doesn't have to match the heading shown at the top of your web page. Search engines usually provide this title when returning the results of a search. You can use up to fifteen words here to describe your web page in a way that will attract visitors. Here's the title I use for http://www.redwall.org: "Redwall Abbey: The Official Redwall Web Site".

META Tags

You can help ensure your web page is described accurately by search engines by adding two <META> tags to the HEAD section of your web page between the </TITLE> closing tag and the </HEAD> closing tag (or the <SCRIPT> opening tag if you've used JavaScript on your web page). There is no closing META tag. Only about a third of web pages on the Internet use META tags, so using them gives your web page a distinct advantage over competing web sites.

The first META tag uses up to 200 characters to give a description of your web page. Search engines often provide this description when returning the results of a search.

The second META tag uses up to 1000 characters to list keywords which describe your web page. Search engines associate these keywords with your web page when they perform a search.

The META tags for "Redwall Abbey: The Official Redwall Web Site" look like this:

<META NAME="description" CONTENT="This is the personal web site of Brian Jacques, the British author of the Redwall adventure stories for young people.">

<META NAME="keywords" CONTENT="Brian Jacques, Redwall Abbey, Mossflower, Mattimeo, Mariel of Redwall, Salamandastron, Martin the Warrior, The Bellmaker, Outcast of Redwall, The Great Redwall Feast, The Pearls of Lutra, The Long Patrol, Marlfox, The Legend of Luke, A Redwall Winter's Tale, Lord Brocktree, Seven Strange and Ghostly Tales, Brian+Jacques">

When viewers search the World Wide Web for "Redwall" or "Brian Jacques" the major search engines should return a listing for the web page which looks something like this:

Redwall Abbey: The Official Redwall Web Site
This is the personal web site of Brian Jacques, the British author of the Redwall adventure stories for young people.

META Tag Generators
You can get online help creating your **META** tags from:

Web Site Garage META Tag Generator
http://websitegarage.netscape.com/P=wsg/O=wsg/wsg/scripts/states/start.cgi?banner=wsg&origin=wsg&page=/turbocharge/metatag/index.html

<META TAG> generator
http://www.websitepromote.com/resources/meta/

Submit Corner
http://www.submitcorner.com/Tools/Meta/

Search Topic: META Tag Generator

Search Engine Registration
Registration is free. Just fill out an online form for each of the major search engines, listed here in approximate order of web coverage:

Northern Light
http://www.northernlight.com/docs/regurl_help.html

AltaVista
http://www.altavista.com/cgi-bin/query?pg=addurl

HotBot
http://hotbot.lycos.com/addurl.asp

Go.com
http://www.go.com/AddUrl?pg=DCaddurl.html

Google
http://www.google.com/addurl.html

Yahoo
http://www.yahoo.com/info/suggest/

Excite
http://submit.looksmart.com/info.jhtml?synd=
zbh&chan=home&sku=ls02&page=form

Lycos
http://www.lycos.com/addasite.html

DirectHit
http://www.directhit.com/util/addurl.html

WebCrawler
http://www.webcrawler.com/info/add_url/

LookSmart
http://submit.looksmart.com/info.jhtml?synd=
US&chan=lshomeft

Search Topic: Search Engines

Submission Engines

There are services on the Internet known as "submission engines" which will register your web page with several search engines with just one submission from you. A few submission engines require only that you place a link on your web page which advertises their service. More often, submission engines will register you with ten to fifteen search engines for free, hoping that you will pay a fee for them to register with more search engines.

The advantage of using a submission engine is that you are quickly listed with many search engines without too much effort. The disadvantage is that each search engine has different requirements which a generic submission may not do the best job of filling. Here are the URLs of some of these services:

Add Me
http://www.addme.com

AutoSubmit
http://autosubmit.com/promote.html

Absolutely Free!
http://www.bizinfo2000.com/submit/add_your_site.htm

Search Topic: Free Submission Engines

Meta-search Engines

There are now so many web pages on the Internet that no one search engine is able to index more than one-sixth of them. For this reason it's a good idea to use a meta-search engine when doing initial searches on the web. It's the quickest way to check as much of the World Wide Web at one time as possible.

Meta-search engines don't maintain databases themselves. When a user submits a search request, the meta-search engine simultaneously sends out search requests to several search engines. The meta-search engine then combines and sorts the search results, and presents them to the user.

Meta-search engines have some limitations. They don't conduct extensive searches. They report only the top ten or so web pages from each search engine they use. If your search using a meta-search engine doesn't return enough web pages to meet your needs, try using individual search engines directly.

Here's where to find some of the better meta-search engines:

Metacrawler
http://www.metacrawler.com/

CNET Search
http://www.search.com/

Debriefing
  (English)
  http://www.debriefing.com/

  (French)
  http://www.debriefing.com/france/

Dogpile
http://www.dogpile.com/

inFind
  (English)
  http://www.infind.com/

  (French)
  http://www.infind.com/infind_fr/index.html

  (German)
  http://www.infind.com/infind_de/index.html

Mamma: The Mother Of All Search Engines
http://www.mamma.com/

Search Topic: Meta-search Engines

Appendix G: Fine-tuning

Once you've created your web site, you'll want to ensure that it's set up to run as efficiently as possible. First, you'll need to check the HTML code and fine-tune it so that it conforms to established HTML standards. Web Site Garage can help with this task. Then, you'll want to see if you can improve download times by editing your images. This is GIF Wizard's specialty.

Web Site Garage
http://websitegarage.netscape.com/

Web Site Garage provides a free comprehensive web site analysis. It checks browser compatibility, readiness for search engine registry, load time, dead links, link popularity, spelling and HTML design. It rates your web page, lists warnings and errors, and indicates what you need to do to improve it. The review is completed instantly and it's free. Web Site Garage also offers several services (for a fee) to fix whatever problems are found.

GIF Wizard
http://www.gifwizard.com

GIF Wizard checks the download time of your web page and estimates how short a download time can be achieved by editing your images, whether they're GIFs, JPEGs, or BMPs. It then recommends how much file compression each image can handle and still retain quality. GIF Wizard will edit your images for you (for a fee) or you can edit them yourself using its recommendations with Paint Shop Pro.

Glossary

ASCII: American Standard Code for Information Interchange, a code for presenting 256 characters of computer input and output

attribute: a word placed within an HTML opening tag which modifies the tag

browser: a program used to browse the world wide web. Netscape and Internet Explorer are the two most popular web browsers.

cache: a temporary data storage area on your computer in its Random Access Memory (RAM) or on its hard drive

cell: the area in a table where information is displayed; the point where a column and a row intersect (cross each other)

CGI: Common Gateway Interface, a protocol used on a web server for scripts which provide web gadgets by allowing information to be transferred from the viewer's browser to the web server where it is acted upon and then returned to the viewer's browser.

clickable form field: a blank space on a web page which displays a scrolling message when clicked with a mouse

co-ordinates: two numbers which indicate a location on an image by giving the horizontal and vertical distances (measured in pixels) from the upper left corner of the image

degrade: reduce

digit: number

dither: to create a color which isn't in a palette by combining pixels of available colors in a pattern which from a distance approximates the color needed

FTP: File Transfer Protocol, a protocol used when uploading and downloading files to and from the Internet

file extension: three or four characters appended to a file name, separated from the name by a period, to indicate the file type (i.e. htm and html areused to indicate an HTML file)

font: type face used in text, such as Arial or Times New Roman

format: a file type, such as GIF, JPEG, or BMP for image files, WAV and AIFF for sound files, or ASCII for text files

form field: a blank space on a web page in which you can type, as with an online form processor, or in which a message can be displayed, as with a message banner

front door: the homepage (welcome page) on a multi-page web site

GIF: Graphic Interchange Format, an image format developed by Compuserve for use on the Internet

hexadecimal: a numbering system based on sixteen digits (0,1,2,3,4,5,6,7,8,9,A,B,C,D,E,F) rather than the ten numbers used in the decimal system

HTML: HyperText Markup Language, the language used to code web pages for the Internet. HyperText means that information on one web page is connected to information on another web page by a link.

ISP: Internet Service Provider, the company which gives you access to the Internet

JPEG: Joint Photographic Experts Group, an image format developed to allow high quality full color photographs to be posted on the Internet.

layout: the setup of a web page; the combination of text, images, and blank space on a web page.

logo: a combination of an image and words, used to identify an organiztion such as a company or a club.

lower case: non-capital letters

message banner: a text message which scrolls across a web page. It can be placed in the Status Bar or in a Form Field.

netiquette: code of good manners for the Internet

palette: a selection of colors available to choose from

pixel: picture element, one dot on your monitor. There are 72 pixels per inch on most monitors.

precedence: priority order

proportional fonts: type faces which use characters of different widths. (i.e. an "m" is wider than an "n", which is wider than an "i")

protocol: a set of rules which decide how computers communicate with each other and with peripheral devices

server: the computer on which your files are stored on the Internet

spam: unwanted junk e-mail sent in quantity from advertisers

Status Bar: the narrow bar which stretches across the bottom of your Internet browser

template: a file which can be used as a pattern for other files

TWAIN: Technology Without An Interesting Name, a protocol used by computers to communicate with scanners

upper case: capital letters

Index

HTML Tags & Attributes

C

caption 42, 73
cell, table 72–75
CGI 92
chat rooms 95
CIRCLE 11, 90
clickable message banners 60
color 31–38
  depth 45
  names 32
  palette 31, 46
column 72
combined hyperlinks 20
comment 77
Common Gateway Interface 92
consistent appearance 86–88
control block 68
convert
  image formats 40
  sound formats 69–70
copyright 4, 71
count colors 43

D

data tables 74–75
decrease color depth 43
definition lists 12
description 106
DISC 11
dither 31–32
domain 18
download time 43–44

E

editing images 40
e-mail, web-based 100
e-mail hyperlinks 20–25
empty table cell 34, 55

F

File Transfer Protocol 18
footer 87–88
form field 57, 59
form processors 94
front door 86
FTP 8, 18, 103

G

gadgets, web 92–96
GIF 39, 40, 54, 66–67
GIF Construction Set 67–68, 98
GIF Wizard 110
glossary 111–112
Graphic Interchange Format 39

guest books 93–94

H

header 87–88
headings 10–16
hexadecimal numbers 32
HTML 1
  comment 77
  tags 2
HTTP 18
hyperlink color 33–34
hyperlinks 17–30
HyperText Markup Language 1
HyperText Transfer Protocol 18

I

images 39–53
  alignment 41–42
  animated 66–71
  aspect ratio 43
  background 54–56
  co-ordinates 89–91
  editing 40, 43–47
  format 39–40
    conversion 40
  hyperlinks 25, 44
  libraries 47, 55–56, 67
  maps 89–91
  resolution 48
  scanning 48
  size 43–44
  spacing 42
  thumbnail 44
increase color depth 45
interactive 60, 92
interlaced images 40
internal hyperlinks 19–20
Internet access 99
Internet Explorer 7, 31, 98
Internet search engines 2, 33, 106–109
Internet Service Provider 7, 92, 101
ISP 7, 92, 101

J

JavaScript 57–65
Joint Photographic Experts Group 39
JPEG 39, 40, 54

K

keywords 107

L

layout 10, 75–78
lists 10–16
loop block 68

M

maps, image 89–91
margins 72
message banners 57–60
message boards 94
META tag generators 107
META tags 106–107
Meta-search engines 109
MIDI 70, 71
multi-column layout 75
multi-page web sites 86–88

N

naming web page files 4–7
navigation 88
nesting tags 3
netiquette 48, 67
Netscape Communicator 7, 31, 98
non-interlaced images 40

O

ordered lists 11

P

Paint Shop Pro 40, 43–46, 89, 98
palette transparency 44
password-protected areas 95
picture frames 42
pixels 31, 44
plug-in 70
POINT 90
POLY 90
protocol 18

Q

quicker image loading 43–44

R

RECT 90
reducing image colors 43
resizing images 43–44
relative address 18–19
rows 72

S

scanning images 48
search
    description 106
    keywords 107
    topic 33
search engines 2, 33, 106–109
    registration 107–108
servers 101–103
shrinking an image 43
site map 88, 89

software tools 98
sound 69–71
sound format conversion 69–70
spacing 3–4
SQUARE 11
statistics generators 95–96
status bar 57–58
submission engines 108
symbols 4

T

tables 72–85
    border 34, 74–75, 78
    color 34
    data 72
    row 72
table of contents 72-74, 88–89
target file 17
template 87
text color 33
thumbnail images 44
title 2, 106
transparency value 45
transparent backgrounds 44–47
TuCows 98
TWAIN 48

U

Uniform Resource Locators 18–19
unordered lists 11
uploading web pages 103–105
URLs 18–19
URL redirectors 96

V

visitor counters 93

W

WAV sound files 69, 70–71
web gadgets 92–96
web page margins 75
web page titles 106
web safe colors 31–32
web servers 101–103
Web Site Garage 110
web-based e-mail 100
WS FTP LE 98, 103–105

Z

zoom 46

Order Our Book

To obtain your own copy of *Dave's Quick 'n' Easy Web Pages* or to give it as a gift, mail your payment (payable to Erin Publications) with your name and postal address to us at the address given below.

We'll process your order the day it's received. Your book will be securely packed in a bubble envelope and will be mailed the next day via First Class Air Mail. (Allow 2-3 weeks from the time you mail your order, to the time you receive your copy of our book.)

The delivered price of our book is:

USA: US $14.95
(US $11.95 plus US $3.00 Shipping & Handling)
Payment via money order or personal check.

Canada: CDN $18.95
(CDN $15.95 plus CDN $3.00 Shipping, Handling, and Tax)
Payment via money order or personal cheque.

Worldwide: US$14.95
(US $11.95 plus US $3.00 Shipping & Handling)
Payment via money order or bank draft.

We don't accept phone orders or credit cards because they would increase our costs and the cost of our book to you.

If you have a comment or a question about our book, e-mail is the best way to reach us. (Sorry, we can't offer advice on creating or improving individual web sites.)

Schools and libraries can reach us by fax at (403) 239-0853.

Erin Publications

82 Edenstone View NW
Calgary, Canada T3A 4T5

E-mail: info@erinbooks.com
Web site: http://www.erinbooks.com
